READY TO WIN OVER WORRY AND ANXIETY

*W*IN™OVER

THELMA WELLS

HARVEST HOUSE PUBLISHERS

EUGENE, OREGON

Published in association with Van Diest Literary Agency, PO Box 1482, Sisters, Oregon 97759, www.lastchapterpublishing.com

Cover photo © Stockxpert / Jupiterimages unlimited

Cover by Koechel Peterson & Associates, Inc., Minneapolis, Minnesota

READY TO WIN OVER WORRY AND ANXIETY
Copyright © 2010 by Thelma Wells
Published by Harvest House Publishers
Eugene, Oregon 97402
www.harvesthousepublishers.com

Library of Congress Cataloging-in-Publication Data
Wells, Thelma.
Ready to win over worry and anxiety / Thelma Wells.
    p. cm.
ISBN 978-0-7369-2825-0 (pbk.)
    1. Peace of mind—Religious aspects—Christianity. 2. Anxiety—Religious aspects—Christianity. 3. Worry—Religious aspects—Christianity. I. Title
BV4908.5.W44 2010
248.8'6—dc22
                                                                2009053954

Printed in the United States of America

10 11 12 13 14 15 16 17 18 / VP-SK / 10 9 8 7 6 5 4 3 2 1

*My prayer is that this book will open the eyes of your soul
and illuminate the brightness of a better life free
from the weight of oppressive worry...
a life that soars upward into joy and peace.*

Don't give in, God wants you to win!

Acknowledgment

My daughter Lesa M. Cohan has been an illuminating example to me of how to give all our decisions and cares to God and leave them there. Her diligent faith and trust in God is a splendid example for her parents, family, coworkers, and friends to emulate. Thank you, Lesa, for being a bright and shining light of inspiration to all of us. I love you.

Your Mama,

Thelma Wells

Contents

Our Journey Together
7

~ 1 ~
Analyzing Anxiety
13

~ 2 ~
The Fear in Anxiety
25

~ 3 ~
The Fight of Anxiety
51

~ 4 ~
Remember This Reality:
God Cares for You
69

~ 5 ~
Remember This Reality:
God Is Able
91

~ 6 ~
Remember This Reality:
Worry Is a Waste
105

~ 7 ~
Remember This Reality:
There's Something Better than Worry
131

Notes
143

Our Journey Together

Now here's something you didn't expect. Let me ask you to do something unusual...but easy and fun: Think about balloons and their characteristics:

- They come in different colors.
- They come in different sizes.
- They float when they're inflated.
- They bring happiness and joy.
- They create a playful attitude; they're fun to play with and watch.
- They represent a celebration.
- They can bounce like a ball.
- They like being chased and run after.
- They can make us smile.
- They can bring cheer in a sickroom.
- They can bring closure to a saddened heart.

But there's more:

- They're fragile and need to be protected.
- They can burst under pressure.

- Their strings can get tangled when they're not guided.

- They can fly up and away, out of our control.

- They can make us cry.

When I see a bouquet of balloons, I immediately see in my mind's eye a little girl, carefree and innocent, loving life, without a care in the world. Suddenly one of her balloons hits something or someone and it bursts. She cries, "I don't want to lose one of my balloons! They're all mine."

Because she's distracted, her grip loosens and another one gets away from her. She tries to catch it, and another one gets tangled in a tree. She's disappointed and hurt and frightened that she might lose yet another balloon. Her world changes from fun and laughter to sadness and hurt and regret and perhaps even anger.

While we're playing with balloons and enjoying them, we tend to forget that they stay buoyant for only a little while and then they're gone. And instead of thinking, *I can get more where they came from* and anticipating the joy of what we can regain or gain, we weigh ourselves down with apprehension and distress.

Many of us right now have lost our balloons or they've burst right in front of our eyes. We've lost our money (pop), our children (pop), our friends (pop), our spouses or hopes for one (pop), our status (pop), our loved ones (pop), our parents (pop), our dignity (pop). We've lost our faith, joy, hope, peace, contentment, security, relationships (pop, pop, pop!).

Now we only have two balloons left—a black one and a bright-red one. We're so down and out over the loss of the other balloons that we're perplexed and confused, angry and bitter. We fume and cry.

And then comes the time when we realize that even with those last two balloons, we're being asked to make a choice. We must keep either one or the other—or let them both go. Which one will it be?

I reject the black one because it reminds me of the adversary who wants to keep me in the dark about the truth of life. He always tries to burst my balloons by telling me lies. He wants me to feel depressed and guilty and shackled with shame. His influence attacks me as he tries to sink me into pity parties, makes me be hard to get along with, and brings out the worst in me. He strives to induce me to make a lot of bad decisions. And when he is successful, I often blame other people for my awful attitude and conduct, another one of his tricks.

So I choose to keep the red balloon! It reminds me of the time I made the best decision of my life. The red balloon represents the matchless blood of Jesus Christ, and it signifies a hope and a joy that will *never* burst, *never* blow away, *never* get entangled in the trees of life, *never* slowly fizzle out, *never* disappoint me, and *never* break my heart.

All Our Balloons

We all have "balloons" in our lives that represent our many joys and dreams and eager expectations. But the experience of anxiety is always a balloon popper. It lets all the air out of the people, circumstances, and events we want to enjoy and experience.

You know what I'm talking about, don't you? That heavy burden of fretful concern robs us of sleep and peace and joy and happiness. Sometimes it threatens to drag us into a dark, uncertain realm called panic and a free-fall fear called terror.

Anxiety and worry aren't fun, are they? No one can possibly like being assaulted by such torments. No one consciously would choose to be worried...or would they? Anxiety is never pleasant, and yet so many of us experience that feeling often. We've been that way before, and we're afraid we'll get that way again.

Is that right where you are now? Are you gripped by worry? If so, please know that I've been there too. Thankfully I've found some great solutions and strategies to keep worry and anxiety at bay. I'll be sharing these as you and I tackle worry and anxiety through this book.

Good News!

Everybody enjoys hearing good news. Right? Men, women, boys, and girls—we're all looking for positive news about hope, joy, peace, contentment, well-being, and wholeness. But we also have issues (such as anxiety) that block us from experiencing those things. Some people face them occasionally; some people face them constantly. Are there practical ways to deal with those issues? Is there help available?

Yes! What do we especially need? Biblical wisdom and solutions to deal with and conquer those negative issues, including anxiety. So please get out your Bible and have it beside you, ready to go, as we journey together. Throughout this book you'll discover Scriptures you'll want to look up, read in context, and study. I'll also be asking you questions and giving you some things to think about. I recommend getting a notebook you can use as a travel guide for our winning over worry and anxiety excursion. When you see this symbol 🥀, you'll notice questions to answer or room to write down your thoughts. I've also included some pages for notes at the end of this book. You can go into greater detail if you choose to use a personal journal.

Are you thinking, "I've already tried looking up Scripture verses when I'm anxious, and that doesn't really help me. Worry fills my mind and drives out anything that's good or comforting. And then I'm even more frustrated." That's okay. I've been there too. In fact, everyone has at one time or another. We all need extra help and encouragement sometimes for pressing forward in God's Word and holding on to what we hear, letting the good news and positive action steps fill our minds and hearts.

I warmly encourage you to especially remember this exciting word the Lord gives to us through His servant King David: "The law of the LORD is perfect, reviving the soul" (Psalm 19:7). And to our anxious hearts, the prophet Isaiah reassures us, "Be strong; fear not! Behold, your God will come...He will come and save you" (Isaiah 35:4)

When you think about it, isn't it amazing that even when we're at the end of our resources we so often drag our feet about going to God for help—to the only One who can ultimately deliver us from our anxiousness? But even more astounding is how God understands our resistance and narrow-sightedness and still provides help for us. After all, He sent His Son Jesus to die on our behalf so we can access His love and strength and help. And Jesus keeps coming to us in mercy to lift us out of our weaknesses and limitations.

I urge you to open your heart, open your mind, and join me in receiving words from the Lord that can help us deal with the issues that want to drag us into anxiousness. No, I can't guarantee that by going through this book you and I will never again experience situations that bring on anxiety. But I do believe we can and will find refreshing encounters with the truth of who our heavenly Father really is and what He's like...and that seeing all this more clearly will help establish in our hearts the knowledge of Him and the freeing habit of choosing to respond to anxiety in the best way—His way.

I'm excited about our journey together and the wonderful possibilities and truths that lie ahead of us. So grab your Bible, get a notebook and favorite pen, and let's get started.

1

Analyzing Anxiety

A lot of us worry that we worry too much. We sense that a big portion of our anxiousness is unwelcome, unhealthy, and ultimately a complete waste of our time. We know there are things we really shouldn't worry about but still do. And yet, at the same time, there are other situations where we instinctively feel it's right to be concerned. The big question? Where does the line between rightful concern and harmful anxiety lie? Let's take a closer look at what anxiety is all about.

Anxiety's Psychological Background

Getting a better grasp on how common anxiety is might help us relax and be less uptight about this negative emotion. We're not alone in feeling anxious. Everyone experiences anxiety. *Everyone.* Yes, some people battle it more than others. I'm sure we all know a few worrywarts, fussbudgets, and nervous Nellies. But the truth is that anxiety touches us all at various times and in varying degrees.

Although humankind in recent centuries has made great strides in reducing poverty, disease, and famine in most parts of the world, and although technology and science have brought impressive advances in our way of life, it seems that none of that has made a significant impact to lessen our anxiety levels. If anything, there seems to be more worry than ever.

Not many decades ago, observers began tagging our modern times as the "Age of Anxiety." It seems that label has stuck for good. We increasingly battle edginess, unrest, ulcers, psychoses, and more. Lots of folks are even worried sick that they worry too much. We are not at peace.

And surely we're not just imagining all those terrible or potentially terrible things we worry about. Why would we? Nobody wants to worry, right? Don't we all have plenty of reasons to be anxious without making something up? Everywhere we look and every time we seriously consider our futures there seem to be plenty of scary unknowns.

In fact, why don't you make a list right here and now of some of the significant things that typically bring anxiety to you and to people you know. I'm sure a lot will come to mind.

🕸 Significant events and circumstances that cause me and people I know to worry:

Now, you might be thinking that perhaps anxiety is a natural and even healthy response for human beings in this world—especially since it's so common. Let's explore that thought for a moment.

🕸 What are the possible positive benefits of worry and anxiety?

If you couldn't think of any, that's fine. Or perhaps you responded with something like: "If I didn't get anxious and concerned about something important, I might not do anything about it." That's a logical answer. And it makes sense—or does it? Might there be a better way to get us to do what we need and ought to do? That's a good question, isn't it? Is it possible that anxiety is primarily a symptom of our weak and sinful nature? Maybe God wants us to replace anxiety with something stronger and more effective...and even more enjoyable. What do you think? Could it be?

Yes, I know psychology tells us that anxiety often functions in the mental and emotional parts of our lives in the same way pain does in the physical realm—it warns us that something's wrong, that something needs attending to. Perhaps it's true that if we were never anxious about anything, lots of us would never make appropriate plans for our future or carry out our responsibilities in the present.

However, a shortage of anxiety doesn't seem to be a problem for most people. In fact, a far more prevalent problem seems to be having too much anxiety. Maybe a better way to put that is that we have too much of the "wrong kind" of anxiety. Even the experts agree that our anxiety level seems to be getting worse. Listen to this disturbing explanation from Dr. Archibald D. Hart, a leading Christian psychologist and dean emeritus of the School of Psychology at Fuller Theological Seminary:

> There is now ample evidence to show that the high demands and stress of modern life are taking their toll on and distorting our anxiety warning systems. Natural brain tranquilizers, produced within the brain to keep us at peace when there is no real threat or to enable us to act constructively when in danger, become depleted in our overworked brains. The result is a high incidence of incapacitating, purposeless anxiety disorders. This, as well as purposeless worry, is what Jesus warns us to avoid![1]

So you and I aren't the only ones who think this world's getting crazier! Economically, morally, culturally, environmentally—more and more reasons for stress and worry keep piling up. Unfortunately, many people respond to this anxiety-generating atmosphere by popping pills. That tends to bring more trouble, Dr. Hart notes: "The treatment of severe anxiety disturbances puts many at risk for addiction to the medications used…Intuitively we know that prescribing massive doses of artificial tranquilizers is not a satisfactory solution." Indeed it isn't.

Besides being potentially addictive, medications are limited in their effectiveness. "Medications are useful," says Dr. Hart, "only if they buy the time needed to bring one's life under control—to master fears and reduce stress and susceptibility to anxiety. In the end, the problem with all anxiety is a problem of lifestyle, a matter of goals and priorities. No matter how effective treatment is, the problem will recur if major life changes are not made."

"To bring one's life under control" and "to master fears and reduce stress and susceptibility to anxiety"—that's exactly what we want to do together in this book. Dr. Hart's view on the limited value of medications is confirmed by the website Psychology Information Online:

> The use of medications for anxiety management is very common, but not effective without psychotherapy. In fact, many anti-anxiety medications produce dependency, and the withdrawal symptoms are often similar to anxiety symptoms. These medications control the symptoms without eliminating the cause for the problem.[2]

When Anxiety Gets More Severe

Psychologists tell us that there's a close connection between anxiety and depression, and that many of those who suffer from depression also battle severe anxiety disorders. (If this describes you, I strongly urge you to go through my book *Ready to Win over Depression*.) Dr. Hart explains this link between anxiety and depression:

> Several studies have shown that those who suffer from depression also have severe anxiety symptoms. Clinically, the close connection between anxiety and depression has been known for many years. The problem is further complicated by the fact that some of the medications used to treat anxiety will aggravate depression symptoms and vice versa. This can be perplexing, even to professionals.

There is an extreme form of anxiety known as "panic disorder." There are also similar "disorders" that go by various names. The people who experience these tend to spend a lot of time worrying about having another such attack. There's also an element of anxiety in post traumatic stress disorder (PTSD), something that's experienced by those who have observed or experienced situations involving the threat of severe physical injury or death. There's also a chronic psychological disorder known as generalized anxiety disorder (GAD), which tends to last for long periods of time.

Some people experience phobias. They might be deathly afraid of flying in an airplane, being in a tunnel, seeing blood, or even being around insects. Fortunately, people with phobias can live a fairly normal life by avoiding the situations that rattle their nerves.

Acute cases of anxiety very often require professional help. I encourage you to see a counselor or physician if your anxiety seems severe, especially if unhealthy coping mechanisms, such as drug taking or self-harm, come to mind.

In this book we're going to focus on the vastly more common experiences of anxiety that don't necessarily escalate into a high, sustained level of panic (although the word "panic" may sometimes be appropriate for what we're feeling).

Is There Hope?

Since anxiety levels keep rising all around us, does our faith in Christ have anything to offer this troubled, nervous, worried world?

Absolutely!

I couldn't agree more with Dr. Hart's affirmation about this:

> Whatever the type of anxiety being experienced…the resources of the Christian life are profoundly designed to help us cope with it. Achieving a balanced life is the ultimate goal. Whether or not medication is used, we ignore to our loss the profound effect that spiritual dimensions can have on our emotional well-being. Prayer and Scripture are more than just spiritual resources. They influence

how we feel, our values, and our priorities. Humans are more than physical organisms, and nowhere does a balanced spiritual life affect us more than in the realm of our anxieties.

✿ "Achieving a balanced life," Dr. Hart says, "is the ultimate goal." In your own existence, how would you describe "a balanced life"? If you haven't achieved it, what aspects do you need to work toward?

✿ Dr. Hart speaks of "the resources of the Christian life" that are "profoundly designed to help us cope" with anxiety. He mentions prayer and Scripture as two of those resources. What are the spiritual resources you can consciously and deliberately draw on as you push forward to better understand and control your anxieties?

Analyzing Your Anxiety

Now let's take some time for personal analysis. (We'll be doing this periodically as we continue through the book.)

✿ At what times and in what situations and conditions do you find your anxiety increasing?

✿ What particular stresses and strains are most likely to cause you to be anxious?

✿ Do you tend to get most anxious regarding yourself or your loved ones?

✿ What specifically do you tend to be most worried about?

Many times, the strains and stresses that bring on anxiety are caused (or increased) by the fact that we're depending on ourselves and our own plans or resources to help us get through what we're facing. Sometimes we don't recognize how much we need help from the Lord and from other people.

✿ Analyze any situations of stress in your life right now. In what ways might you be depending too much on yourself?

✿ What are your most important responsibilities and obligations?

✿ When it really comes down to it, what are you really responsible for? From God's perspective (as best as you can tell), what responsibilities might you need to consider letting go of or asking for help on?

When the Holy Spirit Uses Anxiety

Sometimes, the Holy Spirit can prompt a sense of anxiety within us to warn us about danger or to prepare us for a challenge. One Sunday afternoon I was visiting a friend and admiring her new baby boy. A sudden urgent fear came over me, and I handed her the baby and announced in a frightened voice, "I've got to go home now!" I swiftly walked out, rushed to my car, and sped home. Just as I walked in my door, the telephone was ringing. When I answered, a police officer said, "Your husband's been in an accident, and you might want to come."

Of course I wanted to come! I rushed to the scene. I noticed at once that my husband's car was a crumpled mess. Then I saw George inside an ambulance. My heart was pounding. In that moment the pressure of worry was my closest companion. I heard no angelic voice saying, "Fear not!" If it was there, it was drowned out by the countless questions flashing through my mind: *How badly is he hurt? What if he's injured for life? How will I tell the children about this? Why wasn't I with him?*

To my relief, George had no broken bones or permanent injuries from this accident. He was able to go home with me rather than take the ambulance ride to the hospital. The car was covered under our insurance, and nobody else was involved in the accident but him so he was the only person banged up. All things considered, the situation turned out okay.

My anxiety dissipated. I learned from that experience that a prompting from God can be disturbing, but when it comes we need to pray for His protection and guidance. He will guard our hearts against the trauma to come and any lies the adversary tries to blind us with.

That being said, it is doubtful that all anxiety comes from the Lord or for the Lord's purposes.

Total Freedom from Anxiety?

What is my response to the psychology professionals (i.e., psychiatrists, psychologists, counselors) who state or imply that we can't expect to live lives free from anxieties?

First, what do they mean by the word "anxiety"? There are different kinds or levels of worry, which is something we can see from God's Word. For example, we know there's a kind of anxiety we must avoid by reading from clear passages such as these:

> And [Jesus] said to his disciples, "Therefore I tell you, do not be anxious about your life, what you will eat, nor about your body, what you will put on" (Luke 12:22).

> Do not be anxious about anything, but in everything by prayer and supplication with thanksgiving let your requests be made known to God (Philippians 4:6).

> Humble yourselves, therefore, under the mighty hand of God so that at the proper time he may exalt you, casting all your anxieties on him, because he cares for you (1 Peter 5:6-7).

❀ What would you say is the general tone or attitude these verses display toward the concept of anxiety?

Now here's something very interesting. Did you know that the basic Greek term that is translated in those verses as "be anxious" or "anxieties" is also used by the apostle Paul in the sense of positive and genuine concern? For example, Paul tells the Christians in Corinth, "I want you to be free from anxieties," and then he immediately speaks of being "anxious [same Greek word] about the things of the Lord, how to please the Lord." That apparently would be a good kind of anxiety. Paul also says that single adults are more likely to have this proper "anxiousness" about the Lord's concerns than married people since "the married man is anxious about worldly things, how to please his wife" and "the married woman is anxious about worldly things, how to please her husband" (1 Corinthians 7:32-34).

Paul uses this same Greek word for anxiousness later when he mentions how God has put together the body of Christ in such a way "that the members may have the same care for one another" (1 Corinthians

12:25). This kind of anxious bond of concern and care even goes so far as to suffer for others, as the next verse implies: "If one member suffers, all suffer together."

The same Greek word is used again by Paul when he tells the believers at Philippi how much he values Timothy because he's "genuinely concerned for your welfare" (Philippians 2:20). So here "anxiousness" is a kind of heartfelt attention that looks after other people's well-being.

Of course, Paul was no stranger to this positive-yet-anxious concern. He mentions "the daily pressure on me of my anxiety for all the churches" (2 Corinthians 11:28). As he discusses the heavy demands of his ministry, he mentions being "afflicted at every turn—fighting without and fear within" (2 Corinthians 7:5). "Fear within" appears to be an unmistakable indicator of anxiety. Paul needed comfort—and God provided it, as the next verse tells us: "But God, who comforts the downcast, comforted us by the coming of Titus."

So there were definitely moments when Paul experienced severe anxiousness because of his genuine concern for the people he ministered to. And Paul doesn't seem to be confessing this as a sin; perhaps he's simply showing us that he's human like the rest of us.

Here's one more verse that indicates how Paul didn't always function with a perfectly even-keel sense of peace. Why not underline the key phrase that indicates Paul's state of mind and heart?

> When I came to Troas to preach the gospel of Christ, even though a door was opened for me in the Lord, my spirit was not at rest because I did not find my brother Titus there (2 Corinthians 2:12-13).

❀ Summarize what this verse tells you about Paul and anxiety.

❀ In what ways can you relate to Paul's state of mind?

All these passages from Paul show us that it's an oversimplification to state categorically that any kind of anxious concern is equated with the sin of worry. Nevertheless, I venture to say most of us realize there's plenty of anxiety going around that is unhealthy and not honoring to the Lord.

We can see this contrast more clearly when we consider how Paul's anxious concerns were: a) tightly focused on the well-being of the people he ministered to or b) arose out of the dangerous pressures of his ministry. The more common kinds of anxiety we deal with are: a) self-centered and b) tend to be focused on worldly concerns.

❋ Do you agree with this assessment? Why or why not?

❋ What are the most significant things you learned about anxiety in this chapter?

2

The Fear in Anxiety

Psychiatry professionals confirm that anxiety is closely related to fear. "Fear" can be defined as "our response to a danger that is real and present." Anxiety is more typically focused on something distant or in the future, something that may or may not happen. The concern may continue to be nonexistent, but we still fret over it. Worry is like low-grade fear; fear is like high-grade worry.

Psychology Information Online confirms that "anxiety is directly related to fear of harm" in terms of physiology. As we face situations that threaten our well-being, "these psychological threats trigger a mild version of the fight or flight response that we call anxiety."[1] Let's think about that a minute.

What are the things most likely to cause you to be afraid?

Good Fear

Isn't it fascinating that in God's Word, the mention of fear often has to do with the "appropriate fear of God" rather than the "inappropriate fear of people or circumstances." I venture to say that the most prominent kind of fear in the Bible is this good fear. The fear that comes from seeing ourselves in light of God's holiness as well as His love and recognizing how far we currently are from His perfection.

As we get a better grasp of this—as we start to see God's holiness for what it really is—we may feel like hiding. But the right place to hide is in the center of the pure light of His love and holiness! And at the very core of His love and holiness is our Lord and Savior, Jesus Christ. The "right kind of fear" always leads God's children to the cross. And we need this good kind of fear to keep us from taking God's goodness to us for granted so we continue to be truly grateful for His grace and blessings.

So Much Fear

While God wants us to maintain the right kind of reverential fear that's totally directed toward Him as our loving heavenly Father, He also longs for us to rise above the circumstances that drag us down into anxious fearfulness in our daily existence on this earth.

In every book of the Bible we find people who are worried and fearful about their circumstances and their futures. And we can usually identify with them easily. Why? Because we're so often that way ourselves. What can we learn from the people in the Scriptures who experienced fear? Let's reflect together on some of their anxious and troubling situations. Try putting yourself in the situations of these people to whom God calls out again and again, "Fear not!"

Through an angel, God said "Fear not" to the banished servant-woman Hagar as she and her dying child were collapsed on the desert floor: "And God heard the voice of the boy, and the angel of God called to Hagar from heaven and said to her, 'What troubles you, Hagar? Fear not, for God has heard the voice of the boy where he is'" (Genesis 21:17).

He said it to Moses when an enemy king came to attack the Hebrews in their wilderness journey: "The LORD said to Moses, 'Do not fear him, for I have given him into your hand, and all his people, and his land'" (Numbers 21:34).

He said it to Gideon after sending His angel to recruit this young man to lead the people of the Lord in victory over their enemies: "Gideon said, 'Alas, O Lord GOD! For now I have seen the angel of the LORD face to face.' But the LORD said to him, 'Peace be to you. Do not fear; you shall not die.' Then Gideon built an altar there to the LORD and called it, The LORD is Peace" (Judges 6:22-24).

He said it to His young prophet Jeremiah when He called this man to a lifetime of speaking unpopular words to His people: "The LORD said to me, 'Do not say, "I am only a youth"; for to all to whom I send you, you shall go, and whatever I command you, you shall speak. Do not be afraid of them, for I am with you to deliver you, declares the LORD'" (Jeremiah 1:7-8).

He did the same with His prophet Ezekiel: "He said to me, 'Son of man, I send you to the people of Israel, to nations of rebels, who have rebelled against me…And you, son of man, be not afraid of them, nor be afraid of their words, though briers and thorns are with you and you sit on scorpions. Be not afraid of their words, nor be dismayed at their looks, for they are a rebellious house'" (Ezekiel 2:3,6).

He said it again when His people returned from exile and had trouble getting motivated to rebuild the Lord's temple in Jerusalem: "Be strong, all you people of the land, declares the LORD. Work, for I am with you, declares the LORD of hosts…My Spirit remains in your midst. Fear not" (Haggai 2:4-5).

❦ What root causes of fear can you identify (or conjecture) in these passages? (You may want to look up the passages in your Bible to see more of the context.)

❦ How do these root causes relate to the situations that bring you anxiety?

Jacob Feels the Threat

At last Jacob was returning to his homeland that he'd left as a young, single man. He'd been away for more than 14 years, ever since cheating his brother Esau out of his father's blessing. Esau had been so angry that he'd vowed to kill Jacob, so Jacob had rushed away to seek refuge with relatives in a distant country.

Now by the Lord's command, Jacob was returning and bringing his large family and many flocks with him. But when the messengers he'd sent to Esau came back, they brought disturbing news: "We came to your brother Esau, and he is coming to meet you, and there are four hundred men with him" (Genesis 32:6).

Four hundred men! An army! Understandably, "Jacob was greatly afraid and distressed" (verse 7). In desperate need, he prayed:

> O God of my father Abraham and God of my father Isaac,
> O Lord who said to me, "Return to your country and to
> your kindred, that I may do you good," I am not worthy
> of the least of all the deeds of steadfast love and all the
> faithfulness that you have shown to your servant…Please
> deliver me from the hand of my brother, from the hand
> of Esau, for I fear him, that he may come and attack me,
> the mothers with the children (verses 9-11).

❀ Think about Jacob's situation. What is the root cause of his fear?

❀ How might this relate to the situations that bring you anxiety?

Trapped at the Red Sea

After witnessing the awesome miracles of God's plagues upon Egypt, the people of Israel were finally granted Pharaoh's permission to leave his land. But Pharaoh changed his mind after they left, and he and his army chased after the Hebrews:

> When Pharaoh drew near, the people of Israel lifted up their eyes, and behold, the Egyptians were marching after them, and they feared greatly. And the people of Israel cried out to the Lord. They said to Moses, "Is it because there are no graves in Egypt that you have taken us away to die in the wilderness? What have you done to us in bringing us out of Egypt?" (Exodus 14:10-11).

❀ Consider the situation the Hebrews were in, trapped between Pharaoh and his army and the Red Sea. What is the root cause of their fear?

❀ How might this relate to the situations that bring you anxiety?

In that anxious moment on the Red Sea shores, the message God gave these fearful people is also what He offers us: "And Moses said to the people, 'Fear not, stand firm, and see the salvation of the LORD, which he will work for you today'" (Exodus 14:13).

❀ What is the salvation you desire to see from the Lord today?

A Leader Who Needs Encouragement

Even God's bravest servants need His frequent reminders to "fear not" and to be made fully aware of His presence and help. Joshua proved his boldness and faithfulness to the Lord many times. After the Israelites left Egypt and crossed the wilderness, 12 Hebrew warriors were assigned a scouting trip into the Promised Land. They went and then reported back to Moses and the people what they saw: a good and fruitful land that was heavily fortified and defended. Some of the defenders seemed as big as giants! Of those 12 spies, only Joshua and Caleb were brave enough and confident enough in God to insist that Israel push forward immediately and conquer the Promised Land according to God's instructions. Everybody else got cold feet and quivering hearts. The courage of Joshua and Caleb never wavered.

Much later, after 40 years of wilderness wandering, Moses was nearing the end of his days. Joshua had been chosen by God to lead the Hebrews into the Promised Land. Moses offered these words of encouragement as his assistant prepared to face the powerful heathen nations: "You shall not fear them, for it is the LORD your God who fights for you" (Deuteronomy 3:22).

Moses kept up his encouragement for Joshua in a clear and public way: "Then Moses summoned Joshua and said to him in the sight of all Israel, 'Be strong and courageous, for you shall go with this people into the land that the LORD has sworn to their fathers to give them, and you shall put them in possession of it. It is the LORD who goes before you. He will be with you; he will not leave you or forsake you. Do not fear or be dismayed'" (Deuteronomy 31:7-8).

✿ What do you think might be going through Joshua's mind as he heard this? What reasons did he have for being anxious? What questions might he have after hearing Moses?

Moses soon died, leaving Joshua as Israel's primary leader. In a very personal way, God brought more encouragement to His trusted servant. Highlight all the positive and encouraging statements the Lord gives to Joshua at this crucial time:

After the death of Moses the servant of the LORD, the LORD said to Joshua the son of Nun, Moses' assistant, "Moses my servant is dead. Now therefore arise, go over this Jordan, you and all this people, into the land that I am giving to them, to the people of Israel. Every place that the sole of your foot will tread upon I have given to you, just as I promised to Moses...No man shall be able to stand before you all the days of your life. Just as I was with Moses, so I will be with you. I will not leave you or forsake you.

"Be strong and courageous, for you shall cause this people to inherit the land that I swore to their fathers to give them. Only be strong and very courageous, being careful to do according to all the law that Moses my servant commanded you. Do not turn from it to the right hand or to the left, that you may have good success wherever you go.

"This Book of the Law shall not depart from your mouth, but you shall meditate on it day and night, so that you may be careful to do according to all that is written in it. For then you will make your way prosperous, and then you will have good success.

"Have I not commanded you? Be strong and courageous. Do not be frightened, and do not be dismayed, for the LORD your God is with you wherever you go" (Joshua 1:1-4,6-9).

✿ What do you see as the most important parts of this speech that God gave Joshua? What parts do you think might be the most meaningful to Joshua? Why?

✿ What does this encouragement of Joshua say about the Lord's heart and character?

❧ How do you think the Lord's attitude toward Joshua is similar to His attitude toward you?

"Be strong and courageous," the Lord kept saying. In this moment and in this situation, the cure for Joshua's anxious fear is given as strength and courage.

❧ What do "strong" and "courageous" mean to you? How can these qualities help you overcome anxiety?

strength—

courageous—

Joshua strongly and courageously obeyed the Lord. He led the way as the Hebrew people started their conquest of their new homeland accompanied by the Lord's miraculous interventions.

Even as Joshua was proving himself faithful—as battle followed battle and the conquest of the Promised Land continued—God continued to offer him encouragement. He reminded Joshua again and again, "There's nothing to worry about!" After a temporary setback in the conquest (caused by sin on the people's part), the encouragement kicks in again: "And the LORD said to Joshua, 'Do not fear and do not be dismayed. Take all the fighting men with you, and arise, go up to Ai. See, I have given into your hand the king of Ai, and his people, his city, and his land'" (Joshua 8:1).

Later, the enemy opposition intensified against Joshua and the Israelites. Five heathen kings combined their forces against them. If I had been Joshua in that situation, I would have been very worried. And maybe he was. Let's listen to what the Lord said to him: "So Joshua went up from Gilgal, he and all the people of war with him, and all the mighty men of valor. And the LORD said to Joshua, 'Do not fear them, for I have given them into your hands. Not a man of them shall stand before you'" (10:7-8).

Later, in a different part of the Promised Land, even more kings joined together to exterminate the Hebrew invaders: "And they came out with all their troops, a great horde, in number like the sand that is on the seashore, with very many horses and chariots. And all these kings joined their forces and came and encamped together...to fight with Israel" (11:4-5).

More trouble than ever! And more reason for Joshua to be anxious. So God speaks up again: "And the LORD said to Joshua, 'Do not be afraid of them, for tomorrow at this time I will give over all of them, slain, to Israel'" (11:6).

🕸 Why do you suppose the Lord kept giving encouragement to someone as brave and faithful as Joshua?

🕸 God gave the valiant and courageous Joshua reminders to encourage him. What encouragements does He give you? If you're not certain or you'd like more encouragement, how or where can you get it?

🕸 What encouragements would you most like to hear from the Lord as you face the situations that bring on your anxiety?

Job the Sufferer

In looking at the story of Job, we have an advantage he didn't have. We get to see behind the scenes and know without doubt that the Lord *allowed* Satan to bring suffering into this man's life:

> Now there was a day when [Job's] sons and daughters were eating and drinking wine in their oldest brother's house, and there came a messenger to Job and said, "The oxen were plowing and the donkeys feeding beside them, and the Sabeans fell upon them and took them and struck down the servants with the edge of the sword, and I alone have escaped to tell you."
>
> While he was yet speaking, there came another and said, "The fire of God fell from heaven and burned up the sheep and the servants and consumed them, and I alone have escaped to tell you."
>
> While he was yet speaking, there came another and said, "The Chaldeans formed three groups and made a raid on the camels and took them and struck down the servants with the edge of the sword, and I alone have escaped to tell you."
>
> While he was yet speaking, there came another and said, "Your sons and daughters were eating and drinking wine in their oldest brother's house, and behold, a great wind came across the wilderness and struck the four corners of the house, and it fell upon the young people, and they are dead, and I alone have escaped to tell you" (Job 1:13-19).

In his misery, Job said, "The thing that I fear comes upon me, and what I dread befalls me. I am not at ease, nor am I quiet; I have no rest, but trouble comes" (3:25-26). Job's worst-case scenarios became his reality.

✿ Do you think Job was justified in feeling the way he did?

✷ How might his circumstances relate to the situations that bring you anxiety?

The amazing thing about Job's story is that even in the midst of his suffering, he worshiped the Lord: "And [Job] said, 'Naked I came from my mother's womb, and naked shall I return. The LORD gave, and the LORD has taken away; blessed be the name of the LORD.' In all this Job did not sin or charge God with wrong" (Job 1:21-22). Later Job says:

> But [the LORD] knows the way that I take; when he has tried me, I shall come out as gold. My foot has held fast to his steps; I have kept his way and have not turned aside. I have not departed from the commandment of his lips; I have treasured the words of his mouth more than my portion of food (Job 23:10-12).

When Our Enemy Attacks

There was another fearful time for the nation of Israel in the days when Samuel was a prophet. The Philistines were a constant threat and enemy to the Hebrews. Samuel knew that a spiritual struggle was at the heart of Israel's conflict with the Philistines because some of the Hebrew people were worshiping idols:

> Samuel said to all the house of Israel, "If you are returning to the LORD with all your heart, then put away the foreign gods and the Ashtaroth from among you and direct your heart to the LORD and serve him only, and he will deliver you out of the hand of the Philistines" (1 Samuel 7:3).

Fortunately, this was one of those seemingly rare occasions when the people of God responded well. A revival broke out!

> So the people of Israel put away the Baals and the Ashtaroth, and they served the LORD only. Then Samuel said, "Gather

all Israel at Mizpah, and I will pray to the LORD for you."
So they gathered at Mizpah and drew water and poured it
out before the LORD and fasted on that day and said there,
"We have sinned against the LORD." And Samuel judged
the people of Israel at Mizpah (verses 4-6).

Have you noticed, though, that sometimes when you turn to the
Lord it seems like the opposition increases? Spiritual enemies don't seem
to be easily intimidated. If we finally get our act together spiritually, the
devil often intensifies his attacks. This is well illustrated with how the
Philistines responded to Israel's new devotion to God: "Now when
the Philistines heard that the people of Israel had gathered at Mizpah,
the lords of the Philistines went up against Israel" (verse 7).

This must have been quite a sizeable force of Philistines because
the Israelites panicked. They were afraid and said to Samuel, "Do not
cease to cry out to the LORD our God for us, that he may save us from
the hand of the Philistines" (verse 8).

Even when we get right with God and humble ourselves before Him,
we may still face adversities that cause our anxieties to flare up.

✿ What did the Israelites do that was right when they became fearful?

In this situation, like so many times in Scripture, the Lord came
through again in response to Samuel's prayers:

So Samuel took a nursing lamb and offered it as a whole
burnt offering to the LORD. And Samuel cried out to the
LORD for Israel, and the LORD answered him. As Samuel
was offering up the burnt offering, the Philistines drew
near to attack Israel. But the LORD thundered with a
mighty sound that day against the Philistines and threw
them into confusion, and they were routed before Israel
(verses 9-10).

✿ What big lessons do you think God was teaching the people of Israel (and us) in this situation?

Facing Goliath

You probably know another time when the Israelites faced adversity. Remember the story of David and Goliath? Goliath the Philistine was about nine feet tall. He wielded massive weapons and wore impressive armor that matched his arrogance. Day after day he shouted a challenge to Saul and his soldiers: "I defy the ranks of Israel this day. Give me a man, that we may fight together" (1 Samuel 17:10-11). He taunted the Israelite army...and it worked: "When Saul and all Israel heard these words of the Philistine, they were dismayed and greatly afraid...All the men of Israel, when they saw the man, fled from him and were much afraid" (verses 11 and 24).

✿ What would you say is the root cause of their fear?

✿ How might this relate to situations that bring you anxiety?

When the young shepherd David arrived on the scene—not as a warrior but as a boy delivering supplies to his brothers and their fellow soldiers—he was outraged at Goliath's audacity in defying "the army of the living God." Do you remember David's words to King Saul about Goliath? "And David said to Saul, 'Let no man's heart fail because of him. Your servant will go and fight with this Philistine... The LORD who delivered me from the paw of the lion and from the

paw of the bear will deliver me from the hand of this Philistine'"
(verses 32 and 37).

Young David should have been as fearful as any man there—even
more so because he was so young. But something gave him bold freedom from such fear. And it was something he'd learned while pro-
tecting sheep from predators. Before heading out to fight Goliath he
explained to King Saul:

> Your servant used to keep sheep for his father. And when
> there came a lion, or a bear, and took a lamb from the flock,
> I went after him and struck him and delivered it out of his
> mouth. And if he arose against me, I caught him by his
> beard and struck him and killed him. Your servant has
> struck down both lions and bears, and this uncircumcised
> Philistine shall be like one of them, for he has defied the
> armies of the living God (1 Samuel 17:34-36).

Do you hear even a hint of nervousness in David's voice as he
prepared to take on the giant? And what about when he faced that
nine-foot menace?

> [David] chose five smooth stones from the brook and put
> them in his shepherd's pouch. His sling was in his hand,
> and he approached the Philistine.
>
> And the Philistine moved forward and came near to David,
> with his shield-bearer in front of him. And when the Phi-
> listine looked and saw David, he disdained him, for he was
> but a youth, ruddy and handsome in appearance. And the
> Philistine said to David, "Am I a dog, that you come to
> me with sticks?" And the Philistine cursed David by his
> gods. The Philistine said to David, "Come to me, and I
> will give your flesh to the birds of the air and to the beasts
> of the field."
>
> Then David said to the Philistine, "You come to me with
> a sword and with a spear and with a javelin, but I come
> to you in the name of the LORD of hosts, the God of the

armies of Israel, whom you have defied. This day the LORD
will deliver you into my hand, and I will strike you down
and cut off your head. And I will give the dead bodies
of the host of the Philistines this day to the birds of the
air and to the wild beasts of the earth, that all the earth
may know that there is a God in Israel, and that all this
assembly may know that the LORD saves not with sword
and spear. For the battle is the LORD's, and he will give
you into our hand" (verses 44-47).

✿ In your own words, explain the secret of David's calmness and
freedom from fear.

✿ How does David's example relate to your own situation and your
own capacity to be free from fear and anxiety?

When David Was Afraid

Although David faced the giant Goliath fearlessly, he did encounter
fear many times during his life. He sets a good example for us in handling them because he faced them head on and openly acknowledged
his feelings before the Lord. In the book of Psalms, David reveals his
heart to God and then goes on to reiterate how he trusts God to help
him face the situation and dissolve his fear.

David wrote and sang theses lines from his heart. Why not make
them the songs of your heart too? And as you think about how these
words can help you in your battle against anxiety, respond in writing
to each one.

I lay down and slept; I woke again, for the LORD sustained

me. I will not be afraid of many thousands of people who have set themselves against me all around (Psalm 3:5-6).

Even though I walk through the valley of the shadow of death, I will fear no evil, for you are with me; your rod and your staff, they comfort me (23:4).

The LORD is my light and my salvation; whom shall I fear? The LORD is the stronghold of my life; of whom shall I be afraid? (27:1).

I sought the LORD, and he answered me and delivered me from all my fears (34:4).

When I am afraid, I put my trust in you. In God, whose word I praise, in God I trust; I shall not be afraid. What can flesh do to me? (56:3-4).

In God I trust; I shall not be afraid. What can man do
to me? (56:11).

🧩

Reason to Sing

Through his confidence in God, David couldn't help but sing away
his fears...and sometimes I just have to sing too! How about you? Want
to join me in a song? How about "Leaning on the Everlasting Arms"
by Elisha A. Hoffman?

> What a fellowship, what a joy divine,
> Leaning on the everlasting arms;
> What a blessedness, what a peace is mine,
> Leaning on the everlasting arms.
>
> *Leaning, leaning, safe and secure from all alarms;*
> *Leaning, leaning, leaning on the everlasting arms.*
>
> O how sweet to walk in this pilgrim way,
> Leaning on the everlasting arms;
> O how bright the path grows from day to day,
> Leaning on the everlasting arms.
>
> *Leaning, leaning, safe and secure from all alarms;*
> *Leaning, leaning, leaning on the everlasting arms.*
>
> What have I to dread, what have I to fear,
> Leaning on the everlasting arms;
> I have blessed peace with my Lord so near,
> Leaning on the everlasting arms.

In the safety and security of our Father's loving arms...in that
warm and joyful embrace is freedom from fear! Yes, this is my sweet
joy—and it can be yours as well.

> God is our refuge and strength, a very present help in
> trouble. Therefore we will not fear though the earth gives

way, though the mountains be moved into the heart of
the sea (Psalm 46:1-2).

✿ What song is sounding now in your soul?

A Book of Encouragement

In the Old Testament, the book of Isaiah deals with fear and anxiety the most. It is a treasure chest of encouragement when we're worried and anxious. Listen to these words from the Lord to His people
(at a time of great sin and failure on the people's part), and let these
encouragements soak into your soul. Respond to each one with your
own words of agreement, desire, or even questions for the Lord:

> Strengthen the weak hands, and make firm the feeble knees.
> Say to those who have an anxious heart, "Be strong; fear
> not! Behold, your God will come...He will come and save
> you" (Isaiah 35:3-4).

✿

> Fear not, for I am with you; be not dismayed, for I am your
> God; I will strengthen you, I will help you, I will uphold
> you with my righteous right hand (41:10).

✿

> Thus says the LORD, he who created you, O Jacob, he who
> formed you, O Israel: "Fear not, for I have redeemed you;
> I have called you by name, you are mine" (43:1).

✿

Fear not, for I am with you; I will bring your offspring...
everyone who is called by my name, whom I created for
my glory, whom I formed and made (43:5,7).

Fear not, nor be afraid; have I not told you from of old
and declared it? And you are my witnesses! Is there a God
besides me? There is no Rock; I know not any (44:8).

Fear not, for you will not be ashamed; be not confounded,
for you will not be disgraced; for you will forget the shame
of your youth, and the reproach of your widowhood you
will remember no more (54:4).

Faith That Is Careful and Quiet

While a man named Ahaz was king, two neighboring nations
banded together to attack his country of Judah. When this news was
reported, "The heart of Ahaz and the heart of his people shook as the
trees of the forest shake before the wind" (Isaiah 7:2). That was some
serious anxiety!

So God sent His prophet Isaiah to address the situation: "And the
LORD said to Isaiah, 'Go out to meet Ahaz...And say to him, "Be careful, be quiet, do not fear, and do not let your heart be faint because of
these two smoldering stumps"'" (verses 3-4). To relieve the people's
anxiety, the Lord was asking for a three-part response—carefulness,
quietness, and a refusal to be afraid. That's totally opposite to the

panicky restlessness that usually comes along with our worst worries, isn't it?

✿ Be careful, be quiet, don't fear. How do these three instructions fit together to extinguish anxiety?

Isaiah went on to tell Ahaz, "If you are not firm in faith, you will not be firm at all" (verse 9). When anxiety causes us to lose our hold on our faith, life gets worse. Anxiety can't and won't ever solve the problem. Faith will though! Or rather God will, and that's why we have such great need for strong faith in Him.

✿ Describe the link between faith and overcoming anxiety.

Anxiety acts like a corrosive acid on faith. You don't want your faith to rust out or be eaten away, do you? Of course not! So will you trust in God's love even when you might not *feel* His presence? (We know He's with us always, but we don't always sense His presence. And sometimes it seems we feel this way too much or most of the time.)

Isaiah Keeps Learning About Fear

As more and greater dangers threatened the Lord's people, Isaiah cautioned the people in a way that really opens up our perspective about fear:

> For the LORD spoke thus to me with his strong hand upon me, and warned me not to walk in the way of this people, saying: "Do not call conspiracy all that this people calls conspiracy, and do not fear what they fear, nor be in dread. But the LORD of hosts, him you shall regard as holy. Let him be your fear, and let him be your dread" (8:11-13).

❁ Isaiah said he felt the Lord's "strong hand" upon him. What do you think this means? How do you think it felt?

❁ Have you ever felt the Lord's strong hand upon you?

❁ When we're anxious, how does that indicate we're not much different from those around us who don't believe in Jesus or claim Him as their Savior?

The people around Isaiah were living in dread, and the Lord told them their fear was misplaced. They should instead be fearing and honoring Him in a way that acknowledged His holiness. This reminds me of the words of the Lord Jesus in Matthew 10:28: "Do not fear those who kill the body but cannot kill the soul. Rather fear him who can destroy both soul and body in hell."

❁ In your life, what does it (or will it) look like to honor the Lord as holy and to let Him (and nothing else) be your fear and your dread? Does this replace one kind of anxiety with another? Or is it something else? If something else, what do you think it is?

These words from Isaiah are a prophecy of what believers in the Lord will testify to on a future day. Note how he mentions fear again.

> You will say in that day: "I will give thanks to you, O LORD, for though you were angry with me, your anger turned away, that you might comfort me. Behold, God is my salvation; I will trust, and will not be afraid; for the LORD GOD is my strength and my song, and he has become my salvation" (Isaiah 12:1-2).

Did you notice that the kind of trust that alleviates fear is built on thanksgiving for the salvation God offers us?

🎕 In your understanding of the gospel, how has Jesus' death and resurrection turned away the wrath of God and brought you comfort? (For more information on salvation, check out John 3:16-18; Romans 5:8-11; Ephesians 2:1-10.)

🎕 Imagine that you got in the habit of staying more consciously aware of all that God did through Jesus to save you from your sins and give you eternal life. How do you think that might help make you less prone to anxiety attacks?

In this kind of trust, the Lord becomes your strength and your song—your power source and the theme of your celebration.

🎕 How would experiencing such strength and celebration be a big damper on anxiousness? What would this look and feel like in your life?

When Things Get Hot and Dry

What does it take to have a "fear not" approach to life's anxiety-producing challenges and disturbances? Let this message from the prophet Jeremiah form a vivid picture in your mind:

> Blessed is the man who trusts in the LORD,
>   whose trust is the LORD.
> He is like a tree planted by water,
> that sends out its roots by the stream,
> and does not fear when heat comes,
>   for its leaves remain green,
> and is not anxious in the year of drought,
>   for it does not cease to bear fruit
> (Jeremiah 17:7-8).

Heat and drought—that's normally bad news, but not for this tree! As we think about this passage and its application to us, the "heat" and "drought" represent oppressive situations that bear down on us. To trust in the Lord is like having roots reaching down to an ever-flowing, nourishing stream. This is the person who "does not fear" and who "is not anxious." Such a person "does not cease to bear fruit."

✿ What is the "fruit" you believe God wants to produce in your life?

✿ In what ways can fear and anxiety inhibit the growth of this particular fruit?

Our Savior's "Fear Not!"

We've seen how God's invitation away from fear sounds throughout the Old Testament. Let's move now to the New Testament. In His ministry on earth as the Son of God, our Lord Jesus repeated His Father's "fear not" message again and again.

He said it to some fishermen as He called them to become His disciples after He astonished them with His supernatural power: "Do not be afraid; from now on you will be catching men" (Luke 5:10).

He said it again when He strode across the wind-tossed waters of the Sea of Galilee and approached His disciples: "When the disciples saw him walking on the sea, they were terrified, and said, 'It is a ghost!' and they cried out in fear. But immediately Jesus spoke to them, saying, 'Take heart; it is I. Do not be afraid'" (Matthew 14:26-27).

He said it on a mountaintop to Peter, James, and John after their overpowering experience of witnessing His transfiguration: "They fell on their faces and were terrified. But Jesus came and touched them, saying, 'Rise, and have no fear'" (Matthew 17:6-7).

He said it to a distraught father who'd come to Jesus seeking a healing touch on his dying daughter: "While he was still speaking, someone from the ruler's house came and said, 'Your daughter is dead; do not trouble the Teacher any more.' But Jesus on hearing this answered him, 'Do not fear; only believe, and she will be well'" (Luke 8:49-50).

And on the night when He would be betrayed, the night before He was to die on a cross, Jesus said it to His heartsick disciples: "Peace I leave with you; my peace I give to you. Not as the world gives do I give to you. Let not your hearts be troubled, neither let them be afraid'" (John 14:27).

❧ What force and value and significance does this repeated message from the Lord, His "fear not," have personally for you?

When we're facing questionable circumstances and dreading bad news, we can look to Jesus, the author and finisher of our faith,[2] and hear Him sweetly whisper in our ear: "Don't be afraid, My child. I am with you. I will never leave you nor forsake you." And His message isn't only for us. It's also His message for us to pass on to others who are struggling. Throughout history the Lord allowed people like us, His servants, to proclaim His "fear not!" to encourage those around us and lift them out of fretfulness and fear.

🌸 What persons do you know who are feeling the weight of worry and could use a gentle reminder of the Lord's "fear not"? How will you share it with them?

I thank God often that He's in control of everything so I have "no thing" to fear. I can honestly say that by God's grace I've learned to trust Him in such a way that worry and anxiety don't take control and run rampant in my mind and heart anymore. I've learned to give all my cares and concerns to Jesus, knowing He'll take care of me. No more oppressive anxiety for me! Just thanksgiving for how He has given me freedom from the dreadful weight of fear. I'm not saying I never feel anxious, but that as soon as I feel even a hint of worry or anxiety, I immediately turn to Jesus for comfort, safety, and guidance. His provision in this area is part of the abundant life He came to give us!

🌸 What are the most significant things you learned in this chapter about overcoming anxiety?

3

The Fight of Anxiety

If you've already heard me tell the following story (it's in my book *Don't Give In, God Wants You to Win!*), I trust it will be for you what it always is for me—a fresh and welcome reminder of our loving God's amazingly personal care for you and me. It also points me to one of the best passages in Scripture on the topic of anxiety.

For days I'd been experiencing chest pains and having difficulty swallowing food. I didn't know what was wrong with me, and it made me irritable and hypersensitive. I was crying about anything and everything. I didn't like talking to people. I didn't like going home to take care of my family. I resented all the requirements of marriage.

I was battling some long-held feelings of inadequacy, plus I'd received troubling news about someone I dearly love. All this was pushing me over the brink.

At the time I had a great job as assistant vice president of a prestigious bank. I was also teaching banking principles and procedures for the American Institute of Banking in several locations around the country. I was also a successful community worker and church officer. And since my husband, George, was a great provider, we had enough material possessions to be very comfortable.

From all appearances, my life seemed happy and wonderful—and I was good at fooling people with those appearances. I didn't want anyone to suspect my heart was torn in little shreds and bleeding profusely from anxieties and fears and all the negatives that go with those troubles.

In reality, things were a mess on the home front. I'd gotten confirmation on some hurtful things that had happened during my marriage that caused me to become angry and bitter. I also had to finally accept that I had a child in trouble. I was afraid to talk about these situations to anyone at the church or in the community. Yes, there were many people who loved me and cared for me, but because of their closeness to the situations, I didn't want to reveal truths that would upset them. And my best confidants—my great-grandmother and my granddaddy—had died. I was more lonesome than ever for Granny and Daddy Lawrence. I felt I had nobody to talk to. I had nowhere to run, nobody to hold me, nobody to assure me and tell me, "Everything is going to be all right."

I was reminded of the bumper sticker message that says, "Life is hard…and then you die." I wondered, *Am I dying?* Yet I still kept playing the "I'm fine" game. After crying most of the night for many nights, a typical morning for me would go like this: Six o'clock: get up and clean up, get dressed, put on makeup, eat a little breakfast, think about what needed to get done that day, fill a baggy with ice chips and wrap a towel around it, get the car keys, and start the drive to my job at the bank. And then, no matter how much I tried to keep my hurts from following me and hold them back, I'd start crying. Soon my eyes were red and my face swollen, destroying my makeup and dignity. That's what the ice baggy was for—I'd apply that little bag of ice to my face, alternating from one eye to the other while driving, hoping to keep my eyes from getting puffy and looking like I'd been out all night.

When I arrived, I'd park my car in a covered lot at the shopping center next to where I worked. Then I would sit there with my lighted mirror on and my makeup kit open, trying to correct the damage brought on by the tears and anxiety.

Now it was "happy face" time. I plastered on a smile and kicked my brain into don't-compete-with-work gear. And I spoke to myself— or rather, to my problems. I told them, "Today's another day of work, and I will not take you into the building with me. You will stay in this car. If it's hot, I hope you smother; if it's cold, I hope you freeze to death. But you will not follow me inside. I'll be back this evening, and if you're still here, I'll see you then. Goodbye!"

Off I'd go to start another day of work—and of lies. I was determined to walk into the bank with my secret that all was not going well intact. When people asked me how I felt, I would answer, "Wonderful! Couldn't be better." (Liar, liar, pants on fire!) I was dying on the inside and lying on the outside.

This went on for weeks without letting up.

What Was I to Do?

In those times, during the midnight hours when my heart was breaking, I would read my Bible and call out to God. Praying was a natural for me; I grew up praying and praising God. But now it didn't seem to make a lot of difference. Everything stayed the same, and my disappointment grew and became deeper and deeper the more I thought about my life.

O God, what am I to do? was my constant plea.

How can I make it through this?

Life isn't supposed to be so hard!

I've been a Christian since age four—why aren't better things coming my way? Isn't that the reward for knowing and loving You?

But if our lives are supposed to be free of pain, and if we are never supposed to face hurts and disappointments—the very kind we're so worried about—then surely Jesus would never have told us these words recorded in John 16:33: "In the world you will have tribulation. But take heart; I have overcome the world."

Jesus said this because He knew we were going to go through some awful stuff on our way to glory and eternal life in Him.

If anybody had told me what that tribulation was going to feel like when it hit hardest, I might have said it wasn't worth the agony and done whatever it took to avoid the pain. In fact, when my tribulation was at its worst and as real as it could be, I couldn't bear it. That's why my heart's cry was, *Lord, what am I to do?*

A Breakthrough

After praying and crying, and studying and crying, and praying and crying some more, I finally got a breakthrough. It happened one morning while holding a bag of ice to my face and driving with one hand, contemplating how I was going to dress up my watered-down makeup. I know it was the Holy Spirit that morning who clearly told me to read Psalm 27—and to read it on the phone with my child.

After I got to work and parked, I called my daughter and we read that psalm together. And Psalm 27 was just the word from the Lord I needed to hear! My troubled spirit began to calm down and peace came into my mind because I believed what I read.

Let's reflect on this powerful, encouraging psalm from the heart of David. Remember how we said anxiety is really a form of fear? Notice how David addressed that right away:

> The LORD is my light and my salvation;
>   whom shall I fear?
> The LORD is the stronghold of my life;
>   of whom shall I be afraid? (Psalm 27:1).

❂ Do you agree with this statement: "The bigger our God is, the more real He is to us and the less we'll see the need to be afraid and anxious"? Explain.

❂ For countering anxieties in your life, how helpful is visualizing the Lord as "light" and as a "stronghold"? Why can these be valuable pictures to have in your mind?

David encountered many adversaries in his life—enemies were a real and continuing presence:

When evildoers assail me
    to eat up my flesh,
my adversaries and foes,
    it is they who stumble and fall.
Though an army encamp against me,
    my heart shall not fear;
though war arise against me,
    yet I will be confident (verses 2-3).

🌸 Psychologically speaking, what is David doing to cultivate a stronger sense of confidence in God? How can you do the same thing?

🌸 What are the adversaries and conflicts—present or future possibilities—that are the most real to you right now?

When Jesus went to Mary and Martha's house, Martha was "anxious and troubled about many things" (Luke 10:41). He told her about "one thing" being truly necessary: "the good portion, which will not be taken away from her [Mary]" (10:42). This is the same theme David mentions in Psalm 27:

One thing have I asked of the LORD,
    that will I seek after:
that I may dwell in the house of the LORD
    all the days of my life,
to gaze upon the beauty of the LORD
    and to inquire in his temple (verse 4).

🌸 This "one thing" David prayed for and pursued doesn't sound particularly practical and convenient in our busy lives, does it? But we still should be seeking it. How can you do that in your life this week and this month (and until it becomes a habit)?

♜️ What does it mean to you that the Lord possesses beauty? How relevant is that to the anxieties you regularly face?

David goes on to express his confident faith in God's protection over his future:

> For he will hide me in his shelter
>   in the day of trouble;
> he will conceal me under the cover of his tent;
>   he will lift me high upon a rock (verse 5).

David still expected trouble. And Jesus talked about it too: "In the world you will have tribulation. But take heart; I have overcome the world" (John 16:33). David wasn't nervous about what was to come.

♜️ Envision David's word pictures of the shelter, tent, and high rock. What important truths do they reveal about his essential understanding of the Lord and his relationship with the Lord?

Looking beyond today's troubles, David anticipates triumph and celebration:

> And now my head shall be lifted up
>   above my enemies all around me,
> and I will offer in his tent
>   sacrifices with shouts of joy;
> I will sing and make melody to the LORD (Psalm 27:6).

✿ Think about some of the troubles that *might* come that you're tempted to be anxious about. What personal triumphs and celebrations will you choose to anticipate as God brings you through those hardships?

Notice that David doesn't take God's help for granted. Even after stating his confidence in God's action on his behalf in the future, David prays with deep emotion:

> Hear, O Lord, when I cry aloud;
>   be gracious to me and answer me!
> You have said, "Seek my face."
> My heart says to you,
>   "Your face, Lord, do I seek."
>   Hide not your face from me.
> Turn not your servant away in anger,
>   O you who have been my help.
> Cast me not off; forsake me not,
>   O God of my salvation!
> For my father and my mother have forsaken me,
>   but the Lord will take me in (verses 7-10).

David's example shows us that confidence in God doesn't mean we stop praying for His help and presence.

✿ What do David's prayers for help teach you about staying focused on your relationship with God and your experience of His presence?

Again and again David's heart led him to seek the Lord's guidance. Here in Psalm 27 it happens again:

> Teach me your way, O Lord,
>   and lead me on a level path
>   because of my enemies (verse 11).

❀ Note that last phrase: "because of my enemies." When you're undergoing spiritual attack, why is it especially important to receive guidance from God? What are the particular dangers in those times that you need to be guided away from?

David again is mindful of those who oppose him, and he prays for God's protection:

> Give me not up to the will of my adversaries;
>   for false witnesses have risen against me,
>   and they breathe out violence (verse 12).

Overcoming anxiety doesn't mean David ignores the hardships and struggles that loom on the horizon. But he does express his confidence in God:

> I believe that I shall look upon the goodness of the Lord
>   in the land of the living! (verse 13).

❀ When you think of "the goodness of the Lord," what comes to mind?

David concludes this psalm with an application he wants everyone to take away from his situation:

> Wait for the Lord;
>   be strong, and let your heart take courage;
>   wait for the Lord! (verse 14).

❀ Is waiting for the Lord the same as doing nothing? Explain.

✼ When you "wait for the LORD," what exactly are you waiting for? What do you expect to be different or to become clearer when your time of waiting is over?

✼ If you don't feel particularly strong and courageous, how can you become strong and take courage? What changes might you need to make regarding your attitude and actions?

The last two verses from Psalm 27 (13 and 14) were particularly powerful for me that morning when my daughter and I read through the psalm together. We were reading it in the King James Version, which translates them as "I had fainted, unless I had believed to see the goodness of the LORD in the land of the living. Wait on the LORD: be of good courage, and he shall strengthen thine heart: wait, I say, on the LORD."

I also remembered how Jesus gave us a specific reason for letting our hearts take courage: "I have overcome the world" (John 16:33). I believed it! I knew that through Jesus God would strengthen my heart.

I decided to memorize Psalm 27...and did so. Over time this encouragement from the heart of God has allowed me to trade my tears of anxiety for the peace that comes from Him. I learned that waiting on the Lord means resting in the fact that *He is handling all things according to His good pleasure.* Therefore I need not worry about it. Anxiety should have no place in my life while I'm waiting on God.

Waiting on God also means listening for His voice and doing what He tells me to do with diligence and perseverance.

I also discovered that logic has little to do with waiting on the Lord because His logic may not line up with mine. (Imagine that!) God is the sovereign Lord, and in His sovereignty He has dominion over every thought and deed we have or do. Waiting on Him means to move when He says "move" and to stand still when He says "don't move."

Waiting on Him is consciously and deliberately choosing to "rejoice in the Lord always" just as He tells us to do (Philippians 4:4). That rejoicing includes intentional gratitude. The apostle Paul said, "Give thanks in *all* circumstances; for this is the will of God in Christ Jesus for you" (1 Thessalonians 5:18).

More Help from Psalm 27

Sometime after that fresh encounter with Psalm 27, I attended a conference where one of the speakers shared about her sister who was a victim of domestic violence. (She was eventually murdered by her husband.) The speaker said that God led her to Psalm 27 as a source of consolation. She thought of this psalm as the "abuse scripture" for victims who wanted comfort.

At the time I was concerned about a different kind of abuse. The loved one I was concerned about was trapped in a stronghold of self-abuse. I knew God wanted me to shine His beacon of light into this person's life and to infuse His words of encouragement into this person every chance I got. He also wanted me to know that as I watched this person's behavior grow increasingly severe, I wasn't to worry and become distraught. The Lord was sovereign over the situation, and He would take away my worry. Whenever the enemy of my soul tried to deter me in all this, I had nothing to fear because I could be confident that my loved one and I were protected by the Lord.

Psalm 27 became my shelter in times of storms. It became my weapon so that in every fight I could know I had God's loving protection. He was giving me an "It is written" to fight the heavy pain of my anxiousness—my feelings of doubt and fear, guilt and shame, anger and disgust, sadness and despair. I would recite Psalm 27 and God's peace would come and calm me down. And the Lord did bring us both out of that time of pain and sorrow.

But my personal encounter with Psalm 27 wasn't over yet. A few years ago I was surprised when my oldest granddaughter told me she had memorized it as a result of a dream in which God told her to do that. Recalling the magnitude of this psalm's ministry in my life, I was curious. I wondered in what situations my granddaughter sensed the need for reflecting on that passage. She was "only" a young teenager—but then teenagers are fighting for their lives in a world of deception and evil too, aren't they?

When I talked with her about this, she told me she frequently used this psalm in her everyday circumstances—when she was worried about something or when she had a relational conflict. She said Psalm 27 was her "saving grace" when she felt depressed or angry.

I thought, *What you're experiencing is a preview of coming attractions. God is preparing your mind to be like a computer, able to recall His Word whenever needed. And then you can select the words of comfort from God you need when the big tests come.*

Isn't that amazing? God is so concerned about us that He *prepares* us for battle even before we know a battle is coming! And He strengthens us when we're ready to fight. And that includes the battle to overcome worry and anxiety.

Hallelujah!

Strongholds and Spiritual Preparedness

The battle over worry and anxiety is real. I find it interesting how the apostle Peter, right after telling us to be intentional about casting all our anxieties on the Lord, turns immediately to the topic of spiritual warfare: "Be sober-minded; be watchful. Your adversary the devil prowls around like a roaring lion, seeking someone to devour" (1 Peter 5:8).

There must be a strong connection between getting free of anxiety and gaining a better understanding of the spiritual conflict we're in. What might that connection be? After my spiritual relief and encouragement that was sparked that morning I read Psalm 27 with my daughter, I became more diligent in reading my Bible, doing my best to rightly interpret what I was reading. Before reading, I prayed for God to open my eyes so I would understand and know the truth about what I was reading. As Paul wrote to the Colossians:

> We have not ceased to pray for you, asking that you may
> be filled with the knowledge of [God's] will in all spiritual

wisdom and understanding, so as to walk in a manner worthy of the Lord, fully pleasing to him, bearing fruit in every good work and increasing in the knowledge of God (Colossians 1:9-10).

Among the life-changing discoveries I made was the reality of demons and the spiritual warfare we're involved in against them. In time this knowledge led me to experience further deliverance and relief. We have an enemy who has come to steal, kill, and destroy, and he doesn't want any of us to know the truth about his dirty work. That's why it's so important to pray. We need to cover ourselves with the blood of Jesus to be protected from the schemes of the devil.

Now, you might think that recognizing the reality of spiritual warfare provided even more reasons for me (and you) to be worried and anxious. But don't fear! Instead of cringing before the enemy, we can look to God and sing and shout these words with David:

> I love you, O LORD, my strength.
> The LORD is my rock and my fortress and my deliverer,
>   my God, my rock, in whom I take refuge,
>   my shield, and the horn of my salvation, my stronghold.
> I call upon the LORD, who is worthy to be praised,
>   and I am saved from my enemies (Psalm 18:1-3).

✿ How are the first three verses in Psalm 18 an appropriate battle plan for victory in your spiritual fight? Describe how they will help you.

Cleaning House

Once I learned more from the Scriptures about spiritual warfare, I still experienced periods of discontentment and unsettledness because my problems weren't resolved. But my reactions to those situations changed from anxiety to adjustment, from anger to acknowledgment.

The knowledge I gained helped me look more closely at me, my surroundings, my family, and my friends—and also at things in my life that might be attracting or welcoming demon spirits. I wanted to be "sober-minded" and "watchful" about this, as Peter tells us to be (1 Peter 5:8). If these spirits are intelligent, and they seem to be, they are something to take seriously and reckon with. I certainly didn't want to invite them into my life or make it easy for them to stay.

I got so serious about eradicating anything that was spiritually harmful from my life that I invited my friends over to listen to a seminar about cleaning out the demons and "demon inviting" items in our surroundings. I was surprised to find out how much stuff I'd allowed in my presence and surroundings that *could* (I'm not saying "did") attract demons or make them comfortable. Deuteronomy 7:25-27 came to mind:

> The carved images of their gods you shall burn with fire. You shall not covet the silver or the gold that is on them or take it for yourselves, lest you be ensnared by it, for it is an abomination to the Lord your God. And you shall not bring an abominable thing into your house and become devoted to destruction like it. You shall utterly detest and abhor it, for it is devoted to destruction.

🌸 Drawing on these verses from Deuteronomy, summarize the best attitude to have toward spiritually harmful influences.

During this time I received a call from a friend of mine who had become fearful about some strange things happening in her home. I went to her house, and we walked and prayed through every room, asking God to give us discernment about anything that needed to be discarded. I noticed some items from several islands where her husband had lived before they got married. (I'd noticed them on earlier visits to her home too.) She didn't know what the things meant, who had made them, or what purposes they served. But we felt God directing us to remove them.

Our attention was also drawn to other things we sensed a need to destroy—not to give away, but to burn or tear apart. She'd paid a lot for some of the items, but her safety and contentment were more important than holding on to these things regardless of their monetary value. When we finished praying and getting rid of the items, peace came upon both of us, making us realize we'd been obedient in cleaning out the demon attractors in her home.

Since then there have been other attempts at demonic activity there, but we have learned to pray for sharpness in our discernment and to spiritually clean out anything in our homes that could welcome the spirits of evil. We are also more careful in what we bring into our homes.

My friends and I learned to seek and claim the covering of the blood of Jesus as we asked God to show us anything we needed to get rid of—clothes, shoes, pictures, furniture, knick-knacks, books, magazines, CDs, and DVDs—anything that might be harmful. We took this opportunity to stand up to the enemy of our souls and say, "In the name of Jesus our Lord, we rebuke you and destroy you. For His name's sake we pray. Amen."

Going back to 1 Peter, look again at what the apostle wrote in fuller context. He's referring to more than battling demons:

> Clothe yourselves, all of you, with humility toward one another, for "God opposes the proud but gives grace to the humble."
>
> Humble yourselves, therefore, under the mighty hand of God so that at the proper time he may exalt you, casting all your anxieties on him, because he cares for you.
>
> Be sober-minded; be watchful. Your adversary the devil prowls around like a roaring lion, seeking someone to devour.
>
> Resist him, firm in your faith, knowing that the same kinds of suffering are being experienced by your brotherhood throughout the world.

And after you have suffered a little while, the God of all
grace, who has called you to his eternal glory in Christ,
will himself restore, confirm, strengthen, and establish
you (1 Peter 5:5-10).

Notice how this passage brought together these topics:

1. our pride
2. our anxieties
3. the devil's operations
4. our sufferings

All these things swirl together in the complex environment of anxiety. Why not go back and mark the numbers 1 through 4 beside the lines or phrases in the passage that relate to the four topics?

❁ The process of casting your anxieties on the Lord is an aspect of humbling yourself under God's mighty hand. In what ways are your worries an indication of spiritual pride and self-dependence?

❁ How do you think being anxious plays into the devil's hands in his strategies against you?

❁ How do you think strong faith will help you resist the devil and, at the same time, put a damper on your anxiety?

✿ How does the suffering you've experienced interact with or influence your present circumstances or when you look ahead?

✿ Peter mentions in the middle of our passage in 1 Peter 5 that Christian brothers and sisters throughout the world are suffering. As you reflect on this truth, what effect does it have on your anxieties?

> And after you have suffered a little while, the God of all grace, who has called you to his eternal glory in Christ, will himself restore, confirm, strengthen, and establish you (1 Peter 5:10).

✿ According to this verse, what will God do for you in the future? What do these words mean personally for you? Do they lessen your anxieties? Explain.

Isn't it encouraging and faith-strengthening to better understand what the battle against worry and anxiety is all about...and how God will help you survive...and even conquer?

Checking on Our Relationship with God

Now that we understand a little better the forces at work when we're battling anxiety, let's review our personal situations more thoroughly.

✿ How battle-minded are you when anxiety is trying to drag you down? What can you do about the larger spiritual warfare issues at work at such a time?

✿ How will being more aware of spiritual warfare help you deepen your experience of God's presence?

✿ What are the most significant things you've learned in this chapter about overcoming anxiety?

4

Remember This Reality:
God Cares for You

In the next four chapters we're going to look at four "big realities" that I believe are foundational to a right understanding of anxiety and how to overcome it. The first two realities are affirmations about who God is in our lives. I know you've heard these two truths before, but we never grow beyond the need to understand them more deeply, more personally, and in fresh ways. The third reality is a sobering reminder as well as a strategic reassessment of our situation. And the fourth reality is our pathway forward and upward based on the truths in the other three realities. So here they are—the four realities that relate so fundamentally to our battle with anxiety:

> *Reality #1:* God truly loves you.
>
> *Reality #2:* He's in complete control of your life.
>
> *Reality #3:* Worry is a waste.
>
> *Reality #4:* Prayer and thanksgiving are the most effective replacements for worry.

Will God Really Take Care of You?

Here's the first reality stated more fully:

God really does love me, and
He's fully committed to looking after me.

Knowing this truth is the first step in being fully certain that God will take care of all your needs. Are you entirely sure God will take care of you? Have you let Him know about any questions you have about this? To move forward into greater trust of the Lord, it's important to be totally honest with yourself and fully honest before God about what you are thinking and how you really feel about Him.

❁ In the conviction of your heart, what do you believe God wants for you? What does He want you to experience in this life…as well as in eternity?

❁ How confident are you that God wants only the very best for you?

❁ Are you sure God loves you? How do you know?

❁ How has God said "I love you" recently? And how have you sensed His love recently?

◙ When you're in a troubling situation, what do you really expect God to do for you in that moment or season?

Love That Brings Consolation

When you see something approaching on the horizon that you don't want to be there, that's the time to review what you know about God and take to heart in these words from the psalmist:

> When the cares of my heart are many,
>   your consolations cheer my soul (Psalm 94:19).

Logically, having this attitude may seem impossible. When our inner beings are burdened by a multitude of cares, how can there also be consolation and cheer? And yet it's true! This is another miracle from God that He lets us experience.

❧ What "consolations" from God have been the most encouraging and helpful for you?

In Psalm 63, David shares some of the consolations God provides in our troubling times:

> My soul will be satisfied as with fat and rich food,
>   and my mouth will praise you with joyful lips,
> when I remember you upon my bed,
>   and meditate on you in the watches of the night;
> for you have been my help,
>   and in the shadow of your wings I will sing for joy.
> My soul clings to you;
>   your right hand upholds me (verses 5-8).

✿ What does having a soul that is "satisfied as with fat and rich food" mean to you? Describe how it feels…or would feel.

Remember how Peter told us to cast all our anxieties on Jesus because He cares for us? He's counseling us to let God be involved in addressing our anxieties. Squashing our anxieties is not centered around a technique, a modification program, a psychological procedure, or medication. Instead it comes down to our relationship with the Lord. That's why overcoming worry is not like taking aspirin for your headache or scheduling a physical therapy session for an injured shoulder. For anxiety you need a heart-to-heart encounter with the One who cares for you more than you can imagine.

Here's some great news! God takes on caring for us so we don't have to burden ourselves. That's why to worry is to forget God. Our Father in heaven wants us to *always* stay aware and responsive to His promises and His presence.

The origin of worry usually isn't wrong or sinful. We want to be safe and secure. We want to be taken care of and provided for. We want to be all right. Those are natural, reasonable desires. Unfortunately we face pressures and threats and obstacles that endanger those desires. These "sufferings" aren't fun, and we want to be free of them. It's what we do with that desire to be free that determines whether we are moving into a downward spiral of anxiousness or upward into the loving, compassionate arms of God.

Love Brings Freedom

God wants to give us relief from our anxieties even more than we do. And He wants us to achieve that with a special kind of inner freedom and detachment. The Word of God tells us, "For freedom Christ has set us free" (Galatians 5:1). And also: "Where the Spirit of the Lord is, there is freedom" (2 Corinthians 3:17). Think for a moment about that word "freedom." Consider it especially in light of these words Jesus read from the scroll (book) of Isaiah and His comment afterward:

"The Spirit of the Lord is upon me, because he has anointed me to proclaim good news to the poor. He has sent me to proclaim liberty to the captives and recovering of sight to the blind, to set at liberty those who are oppressed, to proclaim the year of the Lord's favor."

Today this Scripture has been fulfilled in your hearing (Luke 4:18-19,21).

Jesus also said,

If you abide in my word, you are truly my disciples, and you will know the truth, and the truth will set you free… Truly, truly, I say to you, everyone who commits sin is a slave to sin…So if the Son sets you free, you will be free indeed (John 8:31-32,34-36).

✿ Describe the true inner freedom the Lord wants you to continually experience.

Remember too that a life set free from anxiety is marked by peace and also by active effort, determination, and accomplishment. That's what God wants us to be freed up for! *He wants us to be free to work and minister and serve for the sake of His kingdom.* With the shackles of worry cast off, we're free to run the race He's set before us.

✿ Regarding service for His kingdom, what do you think God wants you to be free to do and accomplish?

When we're not fearful about tomorrow, we're free to do God's will today! And in this freedom, we'll be better prepared and better able to do the right thing regarding the legitimate concerns we have (the ones that used to mire us down in anxiety). We'll be free to be guided by the Father through the Holy Spirit, to move forward in His will as we fulfill our obligations and responsibilities.

Love Brings Peace

Anxiety is like a heavy blanket of smog that blocks out the sweet, fresh air of God's peace. Are you breathing His sweet air right now? I know there are moments or days or even seasons in life when we seem to lose our connection with God's peace. But that doesn't rule out the higher reality that God wants us to know and enjoy His peace day by day.

Do you remember what the Lord Jesus promised His followers regarding peace? "Peace I leave with you; my peace I give to you. Not as the world gives do I give to you. Let not your hearts be troubled, neither let them be afraid" (John 14:27). When we're at peace, when we're truly experiencing the kind of peace Jesus is talking about (His peace!), we're secure.

☙ What most often threatens your sense of security in the Lord? Are there patterns of insecurity in your life? If yes, what are they?

Our Good and Gentle Shepherd

In your mind and imagination, picture the message of this encouraging verse about the Lord's loving care:

> He will tend his flock like a shepherd;
>   he will gather the lambs in his arms;
> he will carry them in his bosom,
>   and gently lead those that are with young
> (Isaiah 40:11).

☙ From these images and in your own words, what do you think the Lord wants you to understand about Him?

Now do the same kind of reflection with these familiar words from David. Let every phrase bring a picture to your mind that touches your soul:

> The LORD is my shepherd; I shall not want.
>> He makes me lie down in green pastures.

🎕

> He leads me beside still waters.
>> He restores my soul.

🎕

> He leads me in paths of righteousness
>> for his name's sake.

🎕

> Even though I walk through the valley of the shadow of death,
>> I will fear no evil,
> for you are with me;
>> your rod and your staff,
>> they comfort me.

🎕

> You prepare a table before me
>> in the presence of my enemies;

🎕

you anoint my head with oil;
   my cup overflows.

✿

Surely goodness and mercy shall follow me
   all the days of my life,

✿

and I shall dwell in the house of the LORD forever
(Psalm 23).

✿

✿ In your own words, what is the Lord telling you about Himself in the images from Psalm 23.

Now, apply the same kind of reflection to these personal portraits Jesus gave us:

I am the good shepherd. The good shepherd lays down his
life for the sheep (John 10:11).

✿

I am the good shepherd. I know my own and my own know me (verse 14).

❄

My sheep hear my voice, and I know them, and they follow me. I give them eternal life, and they will never perish, and no one will snatch them out of my hand (verses 27-28).

❄

❄ What is the Lord showing you about Himself in these descriptions?

❄ In the images from Psalm 23 and John 10, what are the very best reasons you see for not caving in to anxiety when it threatens to overwhelm you?

The Lord gave His prophet Isaiah this message for His people: "Tell the righteous that it shall be well with them" (Isaiah 3:10). Do these words apply to you and me? Do we dare count ourselves among "the righteous"?

Yes! Yes, we can...and all because of Jesus. All because of the truth about us found in 1 Corinthians 1:30 NKJV: "You are in Christ Jesus, who became for us wisdom from God—and righteousness and sanctification and redemption." And all because of the truth found in 2 Corinthians 5:21: The sinless One became sin "so that in him we might become the righteousness of God." And all because of the truth of Romans 3:22, where we read about "the righteousness of God through faith in Jesus Christ for all who believe."

These passages show why the message to "the righteous" in Isaiah 3:10 is a word from the Lord for all His children—including you and me! "It shall be well" with us!

✷ What do you think this well-being means for you personally? What does it (or will it) look like?

God provides for all His children, yet by His will He also allows many of them to live in humble poverty. Undoubtedly this is the kind of lifestyle He calls some of His children to—just as it was the kind of lifestyle Jesus and many of the early disciples lived.

✷ Do you agree with those statements? Why or why not? If yes, why do you think God allows a life of monetary poverty for so many… and even calls them to it?

✷ Can you still be confident that God will fully provide for your needs even if He has called you to a season or lifetime of poverty? Why or why not?

God's Goodness and Compassion

How great the goodness and compassion of God! Not only does He love you, but it's His will and desire and pleasure to love you. I encourage you to linger in His love. Let His love touch your innermost being. Let these loving words speak to and fill your heart in a fresh way:

> God, being rich in mercy, because of the great love with which he loved us, even when we were dead in our trespasses, made us alive together with Christ   by grace you have been saved (Ephesians 2:4-5).

> Anyone who does not love does not know God, because God is love (1 John 4:8).

🌸 What do those verses tell you about the One who created you and gave you this life you're living? What special message do they give you for today?

How long can we count on God to keep loving us? David tells us the answer: "The LORD is good; his steadfast love endures forever" (Psalm 100:5).

🌸 Do you believe God's love for you is never-ending? Why or why not? If yes, why is this important?

🌸 Looking ahead, what do you think your experiences of God's love will be like? How does this compare to your past and present experiences? Considering eternity, what do you get to look forward to?

Simon Peter, one of Jesus' staunch disciples, denied His Lord three times on the day He was arrested. Revealing His great compassion and understanding, Jesus met with some of the disciples, including Peter, one morning on the shores of the Sea of Galilee shortly after He was resurrected. After breakfast together, Jesus asked Peter three times in quick succession, "Do you love me?" (John 21:15-17). I believe the Lord is asking you and me this question today. And our answers will unmistakably reflect our level of trust and confidence in Him. My answer would be, "Yes!"

🕸 What would your answer be?

In that same conversation time beside the Sea of Galilee, Jesus told Peter, "Follow me" (21:19). I'm certain that Jesus, our Good Shepherd, also imparts that command to you and me. (And our Lord's every command to us in Scripture is an invitation to be with Him and help Him accomplish His plan. And whatever He tells us to do is doable through the Holy Spirit alive within us.)

🕸 How and where are you following Jesus today? Where do you think He is taking you?

Why not take a moment right now to acknowledge before God that you know He fully knows everything about you—every detail of every need, issue, trouble, and trial? Jesus said, "Your Father knows what you need before you ask him" (Matthew 6:8). Even though He knows what's going on with you, He wants you to experience the joy and privilege of talking to Him personally about what's on your heart. Let the Lord know how worthy He is to be entrusted with all the details of your life.

❧ What do you want to talk to Jesus about right now? Will you do it?

Counting on God's Love

We may try our best to be prepared for tough things to come, but so often we fail once the test really hits us. Even then, however, we can count on God's merciful love that is infinite and inexhaustible. Jesus said, "Every sin and blasphemy will be forgiven people, but the blasphemy against the Spirit will not be forgiven" (Matthew 12:31). So barring one specific act by you, nothing—nothing, nothing, nothing!—will ever separate you from Him.

Are you absolutely convinced that His love for you is the greatest and most rock-solid reality in your life and existence? This is a good time (there's never a bad one!) to review these uplifting words from Romans 8:

> If God is for us, who can be against us? He who did not spare his own Son but gave him up for us all, how will he not also with him graciously give us all things? (Romans 8:31-32).

> Who shall separate us from the love of Christ? Shall tribulation, or distress, or persecution, or famine, or nakedness, or danger, or sword? (verse 35).

> No, in all these things we are more than conquerors through him who loved us. For I am sure that neither death nor life, nor angels nor rulers, nor things present nor things to come, nor powers, nor height nor depth, nor anything else in all creation, will be able to separate us from the love of God in Christ Jesus our Lord (verses 37-39).

Did you get that? There's nothing you're worried about—or ever could worry about—that could ever separate you from God's love and Jesus, your Lord and Savior.

❇ What does this truth mean for you deep down? Write down in your own words your surest convictions about the nearness and permanence of God's love.

Sharing in His Suffering

When you consider your afflictions, and the possibilities of afflictions to come, it might help you to also think about all Jesus suffered. Let this bring you closer to Him and assure you He understands pain and trials.

❇ Talk to your Lord and Savior about His sufferings (you may want to review Isaiah 53). What specifically will you talk to the Lord about?

❇ Is it possible for you to become more like Christ without experiencing further afflictions? Write down your answer and explain your reasoning.

In the Garden of Gethsemane Jesus stared suffering in the face. Do you remember what He did?

> And going a little farther he fell on his face and prayed, saying, "My Father, if it be possible, let this cup pass from me; nevertheless, not as I will, but as you will" (Matthew 26:39).

We need to follow our Savior's example! We want to seek God's will over our own. It's all right to ask to be spared from affliction, but we must also pray for God's will to take precedence...and our willingness to submit to it.

🦋 Why do you think complying with God's will is more important than your well-being and physical and emotional comfort?

Your Value to God

Think about the following verses and what Jesus is communicating about your value to your Father in heaven:

> Are not two sparrows sold for a penny? And not one of them will fall to the ground apart from your Father. But even the hairs of your head are all numbered. Fear not, therefore; you are of more value than many sparrows (Matthew 10:29-31).

When we're worried about our lives, we can lose sight of the real value and sacredness of our lives.

🦋 What is your value to God? How do you know?

The cross of Christ (where the penalty for our sins was paid) and the resurrection of Christ (where we were guaranteed the promises of living in victory over sin and eternal life with Him) are our great lasting proofs of God's trustworthy love for us. Join me in saying, "Amen and hallelujah!" But we also know He loves us and cares about us from other verses and passages of Scripture.

🦋 What are some of the Bible stories, events, and circumstances that have encouraged you and strengthened your assurance that God loves you?

Mary's Good Example

When I think about Mary at the time when she learned she was to be the mother of God's Son, I envision someone who had as many reasons (or more!) to worry as we do. I can feel her uncertainty and rising fear as she realizes more and more that she's going to conceive a baby without being married to her fiancé Joseph. Not only was this going to be embarrassing, possibly life-threatening, and definitely life-changing for Mary, but also it would be totally perplexing because she had never been with a man. (To me it's perplexing *and* mystifying.)

We read that Mary was "greatly troubled" when the angel Gabriel gave her that news (Luke 1:29). And it's no wonder! In her place I would have had a lot of questions, starting with, "How in the world can this happen? What did I do to get in this fix? Is there something somebody didn't tell me about conceiving a baby? I'm a virgin without a clue! And how will Joseph take this news?" Then I'd move on to coping strategies and "reasonable solutions" for what was going to happen. "Can I hide from Joseph (and everybody else) until this incident is over?"

In Mary's situation I might have been drowning my pillow with tears and crying profusely and trembling all over. Or maybe I'd be screaming at the top of my lungs and walking around in circles—dazed, scared, confused, beating the ground, and hoping the angel thing had all been a dream.

Oh, but not the virgin Mary! The loving God of the universe mitigated her shock from this unprecedented news by having the angel

Gabriel tell her, "Do not be afraid, Mary." And why not? Gabriel quickly gives the reason: "You have found favor with God" (Luke 1:30).

Favor with God! Have you ever thought about your trials and afflictions in that light? Is it possible that along with all our uncertainty, God's message to us is very much like His encouragement to Mary? Quiet your heart and hear Him say to you, "Do not be afraid, My love, for you have found favor with Me." And then remember the blessed assurance the psalmist David wrote about: "[The Lord's] favor is for a lifetime" (Psalm 30:5). His favor never ends!

Are you thinking, *Me? I have found favor with God? How can that be?* But it's true! Think about it. When Jesus came to this earth, He needed only one mother, only one woman to carry Him as the Son of God in her womb, and Mary filled that role faithfully as she rested and trusted in God's special favor. And this same Son of God grew up, lived a sinless and perfect life, died for our sins, and then was resurrected so we can know Him personally and receive salvation, so we can receive and experience His very life by faith as He resides within our hearts. What greater favor from God could there be than that?

And you've not only been given the gospel news that tells you all about this, but you've also been granted the faith to believe it and enjoy it forever! God's favor only gets better and better!

Despite what triggers your fears and anxieties, you have every reason to be confident before God as you rest in Him.

✦ How do the following passages confirm that you have indeed received "favor from God"?

> For the LORD God is a sun and shield;
> the LORD bestows favor and honor.
> No good thing does he withhold
> from those who walk uprightly
> (Psalm 84:11).

✦

As far as the east is from the west,
   so far does he remove our transgressions
   from us (Psalm 103:12).

❁

He who did not spare his own Son but gave him up for
   us all, how will he not also with him graciously give
   us all things? (Romans 8:32).

❁

Now we have received not the spirit of the world,
   but the Spirit who is from God, that we might
   understand the things freely given us by God
   (1 Corinthians 2:12).

❁

You are no longer strangers and aliens, but you are fellow citizens with the saints and members of the
   household of God (Ephesians 2:19).

❁

At one time you were darkness, but now you are light in
   the Lord (Ephesians 5:8).

❁

Once you had not received mercy, but now you have
received mercy (1 Peter 2:10).

🕸

A Song from Mary's Soul

Yes, Mary had so many reasons to be worried. She faced much
uncertainty. And yet listen to the song that came forth from her soul
when she went to visit her cousin Elizabeth. The words she sang reveal
what Mary believes about God and His character, His attitude and
actions toward her as an individual, and that she was very familiar
with God's Word:

> My soul magnifies the Lord,
>> and my spirit rejoices in God my Savior,
> for he has looked on the humble estate of his servant.
>> For behold, from now on all generations will call me
>> blessed;
> for he who is mighty has done great things for me,
>> and holy is his name.
> And his mercy is for those who fear him
>> from generation to generation.
> He has shown strength with his arm;
>> he has scattered the proud in the thoughts of their
>> hearts;
> he has brought down the mighty from their thrones
>> and exalted those of humble estate;
> he has filled the hungry with good things,
>> and the rich he has sent away empty.
> He has helped his servant Israel,
>> in remembrance of his mercy,
>> as he spoke to our fathers,
>> to Abraham and to his offspring forever
> (Luke 1:46-55).

❀ Reflect on the words of Mary's song. Which of her expressions and phrases are true for you in your situation at this time? Underline them in the Luke passage and then rewrite them in your own words as personal statements of affirmation and praise to God.

Checking on Our Relationship with God

Now that we've brought into clearer focus the absolute certainty of God's love for us, take a look at your situation more thoroughly.

❀ What most convinces you that God's true desire and will are for your happiness?

❀ Why do you think God enjoys hearing your prayers? (List as many reasons as you can.)

❀ How does the act and process of praying deepen your experience of God's presence and personality?

✿ When God, in His infinite wisdom and love, chooses not to give you something you've desired and prayed for, how does it affect your relationship with Him?

✿ In what ways could this experience deepen your relationship with God?

✿ When God allows suffering in your life, have you ever looked at it as a mark of His love? If yes, in what significant ways have you seen and experienced this?

✿ What are the most significant things you've learned in this chapter about overcoming anxiety?

5

Remember This Reality:
God Is Able

I have an idea. Why don't you memorize the four realities we're exploring? That way they'll come to mind when you're facing trials or undergoing suffering. Here they are again:

Reality #1: God truly loves you.

Reality #2: He's in complete control of your life.

Reality #3: Worry is a waste.

Reality #4: Prayer and thanksgiving are the most effective replacements for worry.

In the last chapter we considered how God really does love us and how He's fully committed to taking care of us and meeting our needs. Now let's explore the second reality. Here it is stated more fully:

God is in complete control of my life.
In the future, when adverse circumstances come my way
(and He tells us they will),
I need to remember that He has allowed them to touch me.
He is totally able to lead me through them
to ultimate victory and wholeness and joy.
He will take care of me now and throughout my future.

God Will Make a Way

"God will make a way." When there's trouble on the horizon, that's a welcome truth to remember and a good remedy for worry. Being reminded that "God will make a way" has brought special encouragement to me at the times when I needed it most.

I grew up in Texas during the era of segregation. When I graduated from high school in Dallas in 1959, I wanted to go to a secretarial school. When I called the school to register, I was invited to come and register in person. But I guess the person who talked with me over the phone and invited me there couldn't tell I was black because when I walked into that office building in downtown Dallas, the atmosphere immediately changed. They told me I couldn't go to school there. They used the "N" word. I tried to tell them I had just called and had been invited to register, but before I could get the words out of my mouth, I was literally pushed out the door. I was humiliated and angry.

Back home I told my great-grandmother (who had raised me) what happened. "Baby," she said, "don't worry. God will make a way. If you want to go to college, God will make it happen."

Granny worked as a domestic for a white lady, and she went and talked with her about my situation. This lady asked me to come to her home, and she talked with me about going to college. I told her I wanted to go to North Texas State College. She offered to pay for my tuition and books to get me started.

God will make a way! He knows the path and the steps that will take us through our future trials *if* we'll let Him guide us.

Wait for the Lord

Instead of hurry and worry, we need to wait for the Lord to tell us or show us what He wants us to do. Remembering that is a strong deterrent to anxiety. You may feel crushed by the weight of recurring problems, recurring sins, recurring setbacks. Each day and each week they hit you, and tomorrow promises more of the same. No wonder there are times when you dread the future. Are you wondering, *Can't God do something about all this?*

Well, can He? Think about this amazing message from God that the angel Gabriel gave to Mary after telling her she would be the mother of the world's Savior: "Nothing will be impossible with God" (Luke 1:37).

🟡 What does Luke 1:37 mean for you in your situation right now?

Sometimes our habitual mistakes, shortcomings, failures, and sinfulness are at the root of our worries. King David knew God could do something about all that—and it's something we can know too. Ponder these words from Psalm 51 (as David brought a tragic sin before the Lord):

> Have mercy on me, O God,
>   according to your steadfast love;
> according to your abundant mercy
>   blot out my transgressions.
> Wash me thoroughly from my iniquity,
>   and cleanse me from my sin!...
> Wash me, and I will be whiter than snow.
> Let me hear joy and gladness;
>   let the bones that you have broken rejoice.
> Hide your face from my sins,
>   and blot out all my iniquities.
> Create in me a clean heart, O God,
>   and renew a right spirit within me.
> Cast me not away from your presence,
>   and take not your Holy Spirit from me.
> Restore to me the joy of your salvation,
>   and uphold me with a willing spirit...
> O Lord, open my lips,
>   and my mouth will declare your praise
> (51:1-2,7-12,15).

🟡 Respond to David's prayer by writing down what you would like God to do (and keep doing) for you regarding your sins and weaknesses.

Remember the Lord's great promise about this: "If we confess our sins, he is faithful and just to forgive us our sins and to cleanse us from all unrighteousness" (1 John 1:9). This is the privilege that is ours in Christ Jesus—and it's available in no other way. With confidence in this promise of forgiveness and cleansing in Christ we can move forward in greater victory over sin and the anxiety that it causes.

🌐 Practically speaking, what helps you most in pursuing a life of holiness and obedience, to "be holy in all your conduct" (1 Peter 1:15)?

Understanding God Better

Since God is all-knowing and all-wise and all-powerful—as well as perfectly good and perfectly loving—how secure are you as His child under His care and protection? When you're tempted to be anxious, you may well be forgetting something about God. One way of staying in better touch with what He's like is to be familiar with His attributes—His character qualities, the things that are true about His personality.

🌐 To reinforce the reality of these things in your mind as a sure defense against anxiousness, here's a list of some of God's attributes. Reflect on these things and then describe what each one means to you. Mention especially how it affects (or could affect) your personal relationship with God.

He is infinite (without any of the human limitations you and I experience).

🌐

He is personal (He interacts with us and wants to have a personal relationship with us).

✿

He is all-powerful and sovereign (always able to carry out His will; He never steps off His throne).

✿

He is everywhere (omnipresent, unlimited by any restrictions whatsoever).

✿

He is all-knowing (omniscient, perfect in His understanding of all things forever).

✿

He is all-wise (always choosing what is perfectly best).

✿

He is perfectly true and faithful (always true in His words and actions and intentions; He's the *only* standard of truth).

✿

He is loving (always giving of Himself to others, always seeking their best).

✸

How perfect and blessed and beautiful and glorious is our God! Using the qualities just listed for God, answer these questions.

✸ Which of these attributes of God are you least likely to lose sight of?

✸ Which of these attributes do you need to stay more consciously aware of?

Knowing Whom We Believe

One of the times when the apostle Paul was suffering as a prisoner, he wrote: "I am not ashamed, for I know whom I have believed, and I am convinced that he is able to guard until that Day what has been entrusted to me" (2 Timothy 1:12). I hope you will ponder this in your heart and let it become your personal affirmation as well.

✸ What do you know about the One in whom you have believed?

✸ What are some of the things He has entrusted to you?

❀ Remember afresh that God is fully able to guard those things. In a written prayer, express to Him your confidence about that right now:

A Change in Security

Perhaps in your past you've been able to find a significant sense of security apart from God in some natural way, such as your good business sense, winsome personality, logical mind and level-headedness, strong sense of morality and integrity, strong family background and heritage, flexibility and adaptability, or your good looks, good health, and high energy level. But now maybe some of that isn't as reliable as it used to be. And as you become increasingly aware of this, you may become more anxious.

To avoid that trap, it's best to make sure we're relying fully and consciously on God instead of on our natural strengths:

> Behold, God is my salvation;
>   I will trust, and will not be afraid;
> for the LORD GOD is my strength and my song,
>   and he has become my salvation
> (Isaiah 12:2).

❀ What natural strengths might be keeping you from enjoying a complete, dynamic dependence on God and His strength?

❀ Write out a prayer to God expressing how you want to be more dependent on Him and less dependent on your own resources.

Confidence in God

We've already touched on the great value of confidence in God. King Solomon knew about this value, and he wanted to help his son realize it too. He wanted his son to stay strong and be protected from fear and anxiety. So here's what this wise man told his boy:

> My son, do not lose sight of these—
>   keep sound wisdom and discretion,
> and they will be life for your soul
>   and adornment for your neck.
> Then you will walk on your way securely,
>   and your foot will not stumble.
> If you lie down, you will not be afraid;
>   when you lie down, your sleep will be sweet.
> Do not be afraid of sudden terror
>   or of the ruin of the wicked, when it comes,
> for the LORD will be your confidence
>   and will keep your foot from being caught
> (Proverbs 3:21-26).

What a wonderful promise: The Lord will be your confidence!

✲ Think about the times when you've been most troubled by anxiety. In those times, what kept you from letting the Lord be your confidence?

Look further at Solomon's fatherly advice. He mentioned "sound wisdom and discretion" as being an appropriate safeguard against anxious fear. He's talking about a high degree of understanding and discernment—in the spiritual, mental, and emotional realms. We know that the Lord, through His Word and His Holy Spirit, is the One who teaches such wisdom and discernment.

✽ What are you doing now, as a regular habit, to ensure that you're growing in wisdom and discernment through the Lord?

So much of our victory over anxiety comes down to the level of our confidence in God. We know we're needy. And when we cast a realistic eye toward the future, we figure out that our needs are only going to grow. We envision so much that could go wrong, so much we might lose, so much we might miss out on, so much to worry about. Will it all work out? Will we be okay? Can we really count on God to come through for us?

God knows all our future situations and all our future needs. He's fully aware of everything, down to the last detail. His Word tells us, "He who did not spare his own Son but gave him up for us all, how will he not also with him graciously give us all things?" (Romans 8:32). If God has done so great a thing as to sacrifice His Son to win for us an eternity in His presence, which He most certainly did, then surely He will take care of our true needs during the rest of our days on earth.

✽ Based on your conviction—in your heart and soul—express how and why the cross of Christ is the guarantee of God's full care and provision for you.

✽ As you look back on your life, what are some of the very best things God has already done for you?

✿ In your heart and soul, what do you know God wants for you in the future? Please explain.

Remember again how Paul, after speaking in Romans 8 of the God who will "graciously give us all things," goes on to paint a picture of "the love of God in Christ Jesus our Lord," from which nothing will ever "be able to separate us" (see Romans 8:39).

✿ Is God's love fresh and alive for you today? Think about it. Why and when and where and how is He living in you?

✿ Is it possible for genuine confidence in God to coexist with anxiety in your heart? Why or why not?

Confidence in God Is More Than Positive Thinking

Is confidence in God the same as simply having an optimistic outlook on life? No, it's not, although confidence in God does help us escape negative limitations in our perspectives on life. Reflect again on these valuable instructions from the apostle Peter: "Humble yourselves, therefore, under the mighty hand of God so that at the proper time he may exalt you, casting all your anxieties on him, because he cares for you" (1 Peter 5:6-7).

To fully cast our anxieties on God, we must first humble ourselves before Him. Did you get that? *We* have to take action. *We* have to humble ourselves.

✿ What do you think this self-humbling requires?

To help you on this humbling issue, answer the next question as fully as you can.

✿ Think about your areas of strength, your proven strong points, talents, capabilities, and capacities. Write them down and then compare your strength with God's strength.

A big part of humbling yourself is allowing yourself to be embraced in the arms of the Lord, receiving His mercy and love, and being completely convinced that He cares for you. Notice how David evidenced this kind of humility when he wrote and sang this psalm:

> O Lord, my heart is not lifted up;
>   my eyes are not raised too high;
> I do not occupy myself with things
>   too great and too marvelous for me.
> But I have calmed and quieted my soul,
>   like a weaned child with its mother;
>   like a weaned child is my soul within me
> (Psalm 131:1-2).

✿ How do you see David's example as the right response to anxious considerations ("things too great and too marvelous for me")?

❄ Practically speaking, what do you think an anxious person can do to "calm and quiet" his or her soul?

Expect the Lord to Come Through

If you feel anxiously helpless about the future or a future situation, remind yourself that *God is able* and that *He will make a way for you* through it. Instead of fretting about what you can't do, focus on what God can and will do in this matter. Focus on *His* purposes and *His* desires and how it will result in *His* glory. Ask, *What's really important to Him in this situation?* Is it the same as what's important to you?

Out of your confidence in God, you can make appropriate plans for the future. Here's a helpful description from the *Handbook of Bible Application* on the contrast between a worried approach to the future and a planned approach:

> We need to keep things in proper perspective. Planning for tomorrow is time well spent; worrying about tomorrow is time wasted. Sometimes it's difficult to tell the difference.
>
> Careful planning is thinking ahead about goals, steps, and schedules, and trusting in God's guidance. When done well, planning can help alleviate worry.
>
> Worrying, in contrast, is being consumed by fear and finding it difficult to trust God. It is letting our plans interfere with our relationship with God.
>
> Don't let worries about tomorrow affect your relationship with God today.
>
> Do you recognize already that tomorrow's difficulties—the things you could so easily get worried about—will provide new opportunities for the Lord to be at work and to demonstrate His power and love?[1]

❆ In the needs and concerns that loom before you, in what ways can you see (or at least imagine) God will be at work in those situations?

❆ What might He be trying to accomplish through your awareness of these things?

Checking on Our Relationship with God

Now that you understand a little better the forces at work when you're battling anxiety, review your personal situation again more thoroughly.

❆ How in tune are you with God's abilities when anxiety is trying to drag you down? What can you remember most about His abilities in such a moment to be less stressed?

❆ Even though God is infinitely powerful and capable, when He chooses not to give you something you've desired and prayed for, how does it affect your relationship with Him?

❆ In what ways could this experience *deepen* your relationship with God?

❄ In what significant ways have you seen and experienced God's strength even as He allows suffering in your life? Are you convinced this "allowance" is in no way a reflection of any weakness on His part? Explain.

❄ What are the most significant things you've learned in this chapter about overcoming anxiety?

6

Remember This Reality:
Worry Is a Waste

Let's recall our four big realities:

Reality #1: God truly loves me.

Reality #2: He's in complete control of my life.

Reality #3: Worry is a waste.

Reality #4: Prayer and thanksgiving are the best replacements for worry.

So far we've highlighted how God really loves us and He's fully committed to taking care of us and meeting our needs. We emphasized also that He wants to take care of us through our futures—and He can and will! Because He's in complete control of our lives, when adverse circumstances inevitably come our way, we can know that our heavenly Father has allowed them to touch us. He's totally willing and able to lead us through our trials to victory and, ultimately, joy and wholeness.

So let's move on to the third reality. Here it is in more detail:

*As I anticipate unwanted circumstances,
I need to recognize that worry,*

in and of itself, is useless and pointless.
It is, in fact, a waste of time and energy.

Anxiety's Trail of Damage

Here's an interesting list from the *Handbook of Bible Application* about the harm worry can cause:

Worry may

1) damage your health,

2) cause the object of your worry to consume your thoughts,

3) disrupt your productivity,

4) negatively affect the way you treat others, and

5) reduce your ability to trust in God.[1]

This is what results when we put anxiety in the driver's seat of our lives. The damages can easily happen when there's something we desperately want, something we feel we desperately need, and it looks like we might not get it. We get worried sick.

Do you recognize the destructiveness of worry? Listen to King David: "Fret not yourself; it tends only to evil" (Psalm 37:8). Worry tends to evil! And yet some people seem to choose and even enjoy being fretful. Their worries are the only thing they want to talk about. They almost seem addicted to anxiety. They haven't faced up to the terrible fact that anxiety severely limits their ability to fully enjoy the life God has given and intends for them to live.

❀ Are you convinced anxiety is harmful and unhealthy? Why or why not?

We can learn a lot about the waste of worry from two very contrasting stories in the Bible. Each story involves a man with two wives.

Hannah Takes Her Worries to God

Hannah was an unfortunate wife because she was childless. Her husband's second wife ridiculed her about this constantly. The husband, Elkanah, treated Hannah sensitively and compassionately, but still this was not a happy household. The other wife provoked and irritated Hannah, and this went on for years (see 1 Samuel 1:7). Hannah finally stopped eating and cried all the time.

Finally she took her worries to her Father in heaven. On one of the family's annual visits to the house of the Lord in Shiloh, Hannah prayed and cried out before the Lord. She was so passionate and distraught that as she spoke to God the priest, Eli, thought she was drunk and rebuked her.

Hannah responded, "No, my lord, I am a woman troubled in spirit. I have drunk neither wine nor strong drink, but I have been pouring out my soul before the LORD. Do not regard your servant as a worthless woman, for all along I have been speaking out of my great anxiety and vexation" (verses 15-16).

This was no small matter Hannah was praying about. Her anxiety was "great." We've all felt overwrought at times, but do we respond as she did? Hannah laid it all before the Lord. Talking to God and then being reassured by Eli that God heard her petition comforted her and released her anxiety. Eli, who recognized her need for tranquility, said, "Go in peace, and the God of Israel grant your petition that you have made to him" (verse 17).

Hannah "went her way and ate, and her face was no longer sad" (verse 18). Peace was in her heart because she'd truly entrusted this matter entirely into the Lord's hands.

God, knowing Hannah's heart and her humility, responded to her "great anxiety" with great grace: "And the LORD remembered her. And in due time Hannah conceived and bore a son, and she called his name Samuel, for she said, 'I have asked for him from the LORD'" (verses 19-20).

When the time comes when you or I can say with Hannah, "I am troubled in spirit," and when we feel "great anxiety and vexation," we can always do what's appropriate in that moment—what Hannah did—pour out our hearts and souls to the Lord. That doesn't mean we'll always get exactly what we're asking for or, if we do, that it will come right away. But if we approach the Lord in the same spirit of trust and yieldedness that Hannah demonstrated, we can be sure that the answer our prayers receive from the Lord will be for our absolute best.

While Hannah was praying, she made a certain commitment due to the root cause of her enormous anxiety. It happened while she was pouring out her soul before the Lord. Her words and commitment amazes me and touches my heart:

> She was deeply distressed and prayed to the LORD and wept bitterly. And she vowed a vow and said, "O LORD of hosts, if you will indeed look on the affliction of your servant and remember me and not forget your servant, but will give to your servant a son, then I will give him to the LORD all the days of his life" (1 Samuel 1:10-11).

Before her prayer for a child was answered—before she had any hint of what God would do for her—Hannah was fully releasing that longed-for child into the Lord's hands. Now be assured she wasn't trying to strike a deal or bargain with God. This was a sacred, solemn vow on her part.

When there's something you or I long for so profoundly that it brings heavy anxiety and anguish of soul, are we willing to totally release the object or objective of our deep desire into the Lord's hands? It's not an easy thing to do, is it? Not when it's something we're so desperate for.

You may remember the rest of Hannah's story. She was good at keeping her word. Once her son Samuel was born, I'll bet she never let that precious child out of her sight at first. But "when she had weaned him, she took him up with her...and she brought him to the house of the LORD at Shiloh. And the child was young." There at Shiloh she met Eli the priest again, and told him, "For this child I prayed, and the LORD has granted me my petition that I made to him. Therefore I have lent him to the LORD. As long as he lives, he is lent to the LORD'" (verse 27).

When Hannah vowed to give her son to the Lord, she wasn't planning to do this only after she'd spent years rearing him to be a godly man. No, she meant it when she wrapped her vow in the words "all the days of his life." Her only time to hold on to her son would be while the child was still nursing. In those days, women usually didn't wean their babies until age two or three, so that's how old Samuel probably was when his mother took him to Shiloh and turned him over to Eli.

Think how cute kids are at that age. Innocent and full of life, enthralled by the simplest things, and running to their mothers when they need comfort, protection, and love. Curling up in mom's lap for cuddles, kisses, and naps.

When I think of Hannah giving up her toddler at Shiloh, I can imagine the scene—her little Samuel crying with arms outstretched as his mother tearfully turns and walks away, going home without him. Can you imagine how easy and natural it would be for her to be worried sick about her little boy's physical and emotional well-being as she left him there?

Moreover, she had turned her beloved boy over to Eli, whose parenting skills might have been suspect. We know that because we read later that "the sons of Eli were worthless men. They did not know the Lord" (1 Samuel 2:12). Eli failed to bring up his own sons in the discipline and instruction of the Lord. These two sons should have followed in Eli's footsteps, faithfully serving the Lord as priests. But "the sin of the young men was very great in the sight of the Lord, for the men treated the offering of the Lord with contempt" (verse 17).

But since that was reported to us later in God's Word, we don't know if Hannah suspected any fatherly flaws in Eli at the time—but she may have. Even if she thought Eli would be the ideal parent-substitute for Samuel, surely there were plenty of little things that brought secret tears to Hannah's heart. Would Eli remember that Samuel needed his favorite blankie at bedtime? Would Eli sing to him every night the way Hannah probably did? Would the priest know little Samuel liked crackers crumbled in his soup and not served on the side? Would he sit beside Samuel's bed when the boy was frightened in a storm or wipe his brow with a cool cloth when he had a fever?

I've mothered three children and tended a passel of grandchildren. Just the thought of handing one of them over to someone else—forever—brings tears to my eyes. I couldn't do it without the kind of superhuman strength and resolve that comes from God alone. Surely Hannah felt the same way; surely she knew God would give her the miraculous fortitude she needed to fulfill her vow to Him and survive the heartache. Hannah did see Samuel once a year when the family went to the House of the Lord, and she took him new robes she'd made for him.

Let's learn from Hannah. Let's incorporate her courage and faith into our lives today as a continual, empowering presence in our hearts. When we face the uncertainties that threaten to terrorize our hearts, let's believe without a doubt that our all-powerful God will get us through the difficulties. Let's know, as Hannah knew, that our God will give us the fortitude we need. Let's praise His holy name no matter what circumstances befall us!

This means when we're afraid that illness will steal our health, or setbacks will take our wealth, or disability will replace our independence we'll choose to cling to the God who helped Hannah give up the child who was unspeakably precious to her. We will know what she knew—that He will see us through the hard times.

When we face irreversible losses or when we have to say goodbye to someone we love, we don't have to collapse into helpless heaps of sorrow. We will grieve, yes, but we will "not grieve as others do who have no hope" (1 Thessalonians 4:13). As believers blessed with the gift of salvation, we know God will reunite us with our loved ones someday in a place where there will be no more tears.

God's Word doesn't depict the scene of Hannah giving Samuel to Eli as a time of despair or anxiousness. Instead, what follows immediately in the story is Hannah's beautiful and prayerful song of praise and prophecy, thanking God for blessing her as He had. Her song begins, "My heart exults in the LORD; my strength is exalted in the LORD" (1 Samuel 2:1). This is someone who has ascended far above anxiety because of her dependence on God and her full trust in His goodness.

Even as a young boy, Hannah's son Samuel "ministered to the Lord in the presence of Eli the priest" (verse 11). And Samuel grew up and became a mighty prophet of the Lord, one who had the great privilege of anointing David as king over Israel—the first in a royal line that would eventually lead to the Messiah. Samuel served God devotedly and selflessly and prayerfully in service to the nation of Israel.

Yes, something wonderful came from Hannah's response to her barrenness. She prayed and put her anxiety into the Lord's hands. And the Lord blessed her with Samuel. And we're told later that Hannah and her husband eventually had five other children (verse 21). How gracious our God is!

Two Women Trapped by Worry

Now let's contrast Hannah's attitude and actions with what we see in an earlier two-wife story. In this one, Jacob was the husband, and his wives were Leah and Rachel, who were sisters. Do you remember their hornet's nest of a household and what caused all the commotion?

Like Hannah, Rachel was barren. Also like Hannah, she enjoyed the love of her husband, and that made her sister Leah very jealous. Rachel was clearly Jacob's favorite wife.

Both these women had desires every bit as strong and anxious as Hannah's. But in the way their story is presented, we see their desires resulting not in selfless, deep-hearted devotion and yieldedness to the Lord (as in Hannah's case), but rather in tension, anger, envy, and selfish scheming. What each wife wanted most was what the other possessed. What Leah craved was Jacob's love, and she hoped she could win it through bearing him sons. She eventually gave him six sons in all (plus a daughter), but we're given no indication of any change in Jacob's affections.

Meanwhile what Rachel desired was children, yet none were coming. Finally she cried out in desperation to Jacob, "Give me children, or I shall die!" (Genesis 30:1). This made Jacob angry. He replied, "Am I in the place of God, who has withheld from you the fruit of the womb?"

At this point Jacob could have wisely followed his father Isaac's example when his wife Rebekah couldn't get pregnant: "And Isaac prayed to the LORD for his wife, because she was barren. And the LORD granted his prayer, and Rebekah his wife conceived" (Genesis 25:21). Jacob owed his very existence to that prayer since he and his twin brother, Esau, were the babies conceived at that time in Rebekah's womb. Isaac and Rebekah probably told that story many times as their boys were growing up.

But Jacob apparently didn't do what Isaac did. Faced with his wife's barrenness, Jacob and Rachel chose to work out their own desperate solution. Actually it was Rachel's plan, but Jacob certainly didn't try to stop it, though he could have. Rachel offered her servant Bilhah to lie with Jacob "so that she may give birth on my behalf, that even I may have children through her" (Genesis 30:3). In time, Bilhah gave birth to two sons.

Not to be outdone, after she quit conceiving Leah gave her servant Zilpah to Jacob for the same purpose (again Jacob didn't decline the offer). This resulted in two more sons.

After all these years of barrenness, perhaps Rachel finally began to be more prayerful about her situation. "Then God remembered Rachel, and God listened to her and opened her womb" (Genesis 30:22). At last she was pregnant! She gave birth to a boy and named him Joseph. This son, finally born to Jacob's favorite wife, would grow up being Jacob's favorite child.

You might think Rachel would now be happy and content. But judge for yourself. Scripture tells us the name "Joseph" means "may the LORD add to me another son" (30:22). One wasn't enough; she wanted another boy. In time God gave her another son (Benjamin). While giving birth to him, Rachel died (Genesis 35:18). Jacob buried her along the road as the family moved from one place to another.

So here was a family with 4 competing mothers and 13 children running around—Leah's 6 boys and a girl, Rachel's 2 boys, plus 2 boys each for the servants Bilhah and Zilpah (who probably weren't too thrilled that their sons were claimed by other women). Can you imagine how rare it must have been to have a moment's peace in that household?

Tragically, the striving and antagonism among the mothers was carried on by their sons, as evidenced when Jacob's favorite son, Joseph, was sold into slavery by his jealous brothers (Genesis 37:12-28).

How different this family's experiences surely would have been if Jacob and Rachel, in their love for each other, had also been able to fully and consciously yield their anxious situation and their troubles to the Lord in self-sacrifice, as Hannah did in her situation centuries later.

And yet God has the final word regarding Jacob's family, just as He does for all of us. As crazy and messed up as this family was, God chose Jacob's 12 sons as the foundation for His nation Israel. He poured out His grace and love upon Jacob and his descendants in a continuing stream for generation after generation after generation.

The anxious jealousies and rivalry that agitated this family's existence are not what any of God's children have to put up with. Jacob as a father had many failings, but our heavenly Father is perfect in His steadfast love and care for us and our families. If we'll fully depend on Him and turn to Him, He will guide us.

Rachel got what she wanted when she bore two sons. As noted, sadly she died while bringing the second one into the world so missed out on some of the fulfillment of motherhood she so craved. And what about Leah? We don't know if Jacob turned to her for solace after Rachel died. Did she finally get the love she so deeply desired from Jacob? Or did he withdraw from her because of his grief for Rachel? We're not told clearly. But Leah died before Jacob, and when Jacob was nearing death, he directed his sons to bury him in the same cave where his parents, grandparents, and Leah were buried (Genesis 49:29-32).

Rachel and Leah thought they knew what was best for themselves. They decided what they needed to make themselves happy, and they were anxious to obtain it. God apparently had other ideas. He gave them many blessings, but not the blessing each of them hoped for—or at least not in the way each person had pictured it.

God Keeps Giving Amazing Goodness

Leah and Rachel endured heartache, hatred, and upheaval, and their sons carried those problems into their adulthoods. Yet one of the most profound lessons of Scripture would come from that family's tremendous problems. After his brothers sold Joseph into slavery, this firstborn son of Rachel and Jacob ended up in Egypt, where, after surviving his own set of difficulties and challenges, he became a trusted official in Pharaoh's government.

Later, when a vast famine came upon the entire region, Joseph's brothers were forced to seek relief from—guess who!—that very official in Egypt. They didn't recognize Joseph, but he knew immediately who they were. Granted, he made them jump through all sorts of hoops before he finally helped them, but he did help them. Eventually he told them who he was, and as they cowered in fear that he would wreak justice upon them, he extended grace, telling them, "You meant evil against me, but God meant it for good" (Genesis 50:20).

Think of all the broken hearts in this family and how God used what seemed to be impossible situations to bring about amazing miracles. When I get disheartened and think a situation is impossible, I remember how God used other impossible situations to work His will. I then resolve to strengthen and stand firm in my hope and my faith in God. Amazing goodness can come from bewildering problems, impossible challenges, and broken hearts. And as we learn to see the big picture, we will start to see how little reason we really have to worry.

When hardships threaten to hit, when our hearts threaten to break, let's resolve to learn through our anxieties. Let's ask God what He's trying to show us, what He's trying to teach us, and listen carefully for His guidance. Sometimes the answer might become immediately clear. Sometimes we may not realize what God is trying to teach us until weeks or even years have gone by. We may not know until we get to heaven and can ask God face-to-face.

Meanwhile, whether or not the specific lesson is immediately discernible, whether or not our pathway through the looming darkness is yet clear, we need to let our troubled hearts send us into God's loving embrace, knowing that He will make a way for us.

Isolation

Another aspect of the wastefulness of worry is isolation. In a real sense, our anxieties draw us away from God, but they also can draw us away from ourselves—from a realistic understanding of ourselves and our present conditions. Anxiety keeps us from living in the now and in the truth.

❈ Right now, in this moment of time, what realities are most significant to you?

❈ Do you sense the reality of God's presence in those realities? That everything is before Him? Write down your thoughts about this.

When we're anxiously preoccupied with tomorrow, our worries can create illusions. We become isolated from our true spiritual self that has been born anew through the Holy Spirit's work within us. In the busy, fretful clutter of outward concerns we can lose touch with our inner self, "the new self, created after the likeness of God in true righteousness and holiness" (Ephesians 4:24). What a tragedy.

❈ How does anxiety tend to give you a distorted view of your true self as recreated by God through your redemption in Christ?

Read this encouraging passage that reminds us of the salvation miracle the Lord has accomplished in our lives:

> When the goodness and loving kindness of God our Savior appeared, he saved us, not because of works done by us in righteousness, but according to his own mercy, by the washing of regeneration and renewal of the Holy Spirit, whom

he poured out on us richly through Jesus Christ our Savior, so that being justified by his grace we might become heirs according to the hope of eternal life (Titus 3:4-7).

✿ What important truths do you see in this passage that will help you overcome anxiety by recognizing the truth about yourself?

Jesus Addresses Anxiety

How does Jesus view anxiety in our lives? Does He see worry as one of our worst enemies? Or relatively speaking—all things considered—is it only a minor irritant? The topic of anxiety is something Jesus gave a lot of attention to in His famous Sermon on the Mount (Matthew 5–7). Let's give it our attention as well, and study His words there very closely.

Our Savior starts His focus on worry with a command about something we are *not* to do: "Therefore I tell you, *do not be anxious* about your life, what you will eat or what you will drink, nor about your body, what you will put on" (Matthew 6:25).

Remember that all our Lord's commands are not burdensome or oppressive. They are, rather, our invitation to enjoy a higher and better life. Our loving Lord and Savior is inviting us to live anxiety-free when it comes to certain aspects of our existence.

✿ According to Matthew 6:25, which aspects of our existence does Jesus invite us to not worry about?

✿ Would you say these aspects of life fall under the category of "necessities," "luxuries," or something else entirely? Explain.

Jesus then asks His listeners a series of questions. Here's the first: "Is not life more than food, and the body more than clothing?" (verse 25).

✿ All of us would most likely answer yes to that question. Why would yes be your answer? What is your life? And what connection does that reality have with reducing your anxiety?

Jesus tells us to look around as He asks another question: "Look at the birds of the air: they neither sow nor reap nor gather into barns, and yet your heavenly Father feeds them. Are you not of more value than they?" (verse 26).

Again, our answer to that would surely be yes. However, there are some secularists who would argue that a human being has no more inherent value than anything else found on this earth.

✿ How would you respond to such an argument?

Some people who read Matthew 6:25 ask, "Is the Bible telling us it's okay to be lazy and apathetic? Can we forget about working hard?"

✿ Other than the fact they are forgetting that birds expend a lot of effort and time getting the food God provides, how would you respond to such a question? (Colossians 3:23 might help you with your answer: "Whatever you do, work heartily, as for the Lord and not for men.")

Next comes this question from Jesus: "And which of you by being anxious can add a single hour to his span of life?" (Matthew 6:27).

The fact is, the more you worry, the shorter your life is likely to be. (This has been scientifically proven.) Although scientists and medical professionals labor hard and often heroically to extend human life, ultimately any such extensions are limited and will always lie entirely within what God sovereignly allows. This is a bit of a mystery. The free will God graciously gives us means our actions can diminish the quality of our lives and possibly the quantity. But even then, when our God-appointed moment comes to die nothing can prevent it.

✿ Do you agree or disagree with that last sentence? Why or why not?

Jesus then focuses especially on our need for clothes (and as someone who enjoys dressing attractively, this one catches my attention):

> And why are you anxious about clothing? Consider the lilies of the field, how they grow: they neither toil nor spin, yet I tell you, even Solomon in all his glory was not arrayed like one of these. But if God so clothes the grass of the field, which today is alive and tomorrow is thrown into the oven, will he not much more clothe you, O you of little faith? (verses 28-30).

Unlike the birds, which don't worry but still work hard, the flowers neither worry nor work. And yet how lavishly fine is their attire!

✿ What does the beauty of the flowers tell you about God and His provision?

Look again at that last sentence, where Jesus calls His hearers "O you of little faith."

✖ Why do you think Jesus brings faith into this discussion?

Jesus repeats and expands His earlier invitation: "Therefore do not be anxious, saying, 'What shall we eat?' or 'What shall we drink?' or 'What shall we wear?' For the Gentiles seek after all these things, and your heavenly Father knows that you need them all" (verses 31-32). What a welcome reminder! Our Father knows all that we need.

✖ What kind of attitude are you conveying toward God when you say or think anxiously, "What am I going to eat?" or "What am I going to wear?" or "How will I ever survive?"

✖ If God knows your needs—and He does, and if He's your heavenly Father with full responsibility for your care—which He is, what does this mean for you personally?

✖ Think about your most pressing physical needs (or those of your loved ones). List the needs you know your heavenly Father knows about.

While the nonbelievers in this world are busy chasing after the fulfillment of their physical needs, Jesus tells His followers to deliberately pursue something else: "Seek first the kingdom of God and his righteousness, and all these things will be added to you" (verse 33).

Jesus is giving us a way to guarantee that our needs will be met. We just have to seek the right things.

Perhaps the main point of the kingdom is that the kingdom of God represents the authority of His Lordship in us. He is the righteous King who grants to His children everything it takes to live lives free from worry and anxiety. Christians don't have to grab or go after material things or shallow goodies. We can look confidently to God for all our physical, emotional, financial, relational, and spiritual needs. He will always supply them according to His good pleasure and perfect plan for us.

❀ "Seek first the kingdom of God and his righteousness." Is that hard for you to do? In other words, is it easy or more like a grueling initiation process into a stronger relationship with the Lord?

❀ When you are tempted to worry about something, what can you do to shift your focus from anxiety to the pursuit of God's kingdom and His righteousness?

Here are some additional passages that help paint a picture of God's kingdom:

> The kingdom of heaven is like treasure hidden in a field, which a man found and covered up. Then in his joy he goes and sells all that he has and buys that field. Again, the kingdom of heaven is like a merchant in search of fine pearls, who, on finding one pearl of great value, went and sold all that he had and bought it (Matthew 13:44-46).

> The kingdom of God is not a matter of eating and drinking but of righteousness and peace and joy in the Holy Spirit (Romans 14:17).

There are also many passages that reveal more about our seeking righteousness, such as these:

> Blessed are those who hunger and thirst for righteousness, for they shall be satisfied (Matthew 5:6).

> According to [God's] promise we are waiting for new heavens and a new earth in which righteousness dwells (2 Peter 3:13).

> As for me, I shall behold your face in righteousness; when I awake, I shall be satisfied with your likeness (Psalm 17:15).

> [The Lord] leads me in paths of righteousness for his name's sake (Psalm 23:3).

✖ As you think about the message of these passages, what about God's kingdom and His righteousness make you want to pursue them?

When we actively obey the invitation (command) to seek God's kingdom and His righteousness, one big reason for not getting anxious about the earthly stuff we need is that we won't have as much time to get anxious. We'll be too busy going after our God-given goals—the goals that have eternal relevance.

In concluding this section on worry, Jesus repeats His earlier invitation for us, and gives us yet another reason for obeying it: "Therefore do not be anxious about tomorrow, for tomorrow will be anxious for itself. Sufficient for the day is its own trouble" (Matthew 6:34).

This moment right now has plenty of challenges and demands calling for our time and attention. We don't need to look to the future to find any more. That seems like common sense, doesn't it? And yet we often look forward and anticipate troubles, don't we? Our lives need to be lived in the present.

❋ Right now—today, before you fall asleep tonight—what are the challenges and tasks and responsibilities requiring your efforts and time (in addition to your involvement with growing spiritually through this book)?

Our heavenly Father, in His goodness and grace, gives each of us a daily supply of energy and time. Will we spend it on the tasks at hand, the things He has set before us? Or will we waste them by worrying about the future?

More Reasons to Not Be Anxious

There's yet one more thing we need to observe closely in this famous "worry" section found in Matthew 6. And to do so we need to go all the way back to the beginning of the section. Jesus said, "Therefore I tell you, do not be anxious about your life" (Matthew 6:25).

Notice that very first word: "therefore." This word connects our Savior's teaching on anxiety with what He had been just discussing. And what was He speaking about? Let's look back at the preceding six verses and see. The first verses we'll look at begin with another invitation (command) from Jesus:

> Do not lay up for yourselves treasures on earth, where moth and rust destroy and where thieves break in and steal, but lay up for yourselves treasures in heaven, where neither moth nor rust destroys and where thieves do not break in and steal. For where your treasure is, there your heart will be also (6:19-21).

❋ How will this teaching of Jesus' help you overcome anxiety?

✿ In the last sentence of that passage, Jesus emphasizes our hearts. In what ways would you say the presence or absence of anxiety is essentially a matter of the heart?

Next Jesus speaks of light and darkness:

> The eye is the lamp of the body. So, if your eye is healthy, your whole body will be full of light, but if your eye is bad, your whole body will be full of darkness. If then the light in you is darkness, how great is the darkness! (verses 22-23).

✿ If your outlook and perspective on life (your "eye") is spiritually sound so your inner being is enlightened, how will this help damper anxiety?

✿ Why do you think "spiritual darkness" might cause worry to thrive and multiply?

Now Jesus turns to who we serve:

> No one can serve two masters, for either he will hate the one and love the other, or he will be devoted to the one and despise the other. You cannot serve God and money (verse 24).

✿ How might "serving" money increase your worries?

❧ How does actively serving God decrease your worries?

Slow Suffocation

We discover more about worry in the parable Jesus told about a sower (representing a person sharing the gospel) and his seed (representing God's Word) and the different soils (representing the degrees of receptivity in people's hearts). In that parable, recorded in Matthew 13:18-23, Jesus points out how "the cares of the world" are like thorns. They choke out God's Word and keep it from maturing. The Greek word translated in this parable as "cares" is the same word translated elsewhere in the New Testament as "anxieties." Jesus is talking about the things of the world that weigh us down with anxious concern. Here's how it's expressed in three of the Gospels:

> As for what was sown among thorns, this is the one who hears the word, but the cares of the world and the deceitfulness of riches choke the word, and it proves unfruitful (Matthew 13:22).

> The cares of the world and the deceitfulness of riches and the desires for other things enter in and choke the word, and it proves unfruitful (Mark 4:19).

> And as for what fell among the thorns, they are those who hear, but as they go on their way they are choked by the cares and riches and pleasures of life, and their fruit does not mature (Luke 8:14).

Yep, anxiety has a choking effect. It suffocates us. Think about it. If you feel like you aren't getting enough "air" to breathe—spiritually, emotionally, mentally—maybe you need an anxiety checkup. Maybe you have anxieties blocking your "breathing passages."

Did you also notice how Jesus associates anxiety with "the deceitfulness of riches" and the "riches and pleasures of life"?

✖ What connection do you see between these things and anxiety?

✖ Describe the "choking" effect of anxieties that you've seen in your life and the lives of some of the people you know.

Jesus also uses the words "cares of this life" when issuing a warning about the coming day of God's judgment:

> Watch yourselves lest your hearts be weighed down with dissipation and drunkenness and cares of this life, and that day come upon you suddenly like a trap. For it will come upon all who dwell on the face of the whole earth (Luke 21:34-35).

Jesus is associating anxieties with "drunkenness" and "dissipation." Think of a painful hangover or the pain of overdoing something to the point that your body complains. He warns that the "cares [anxieties] of this life" are something that weighs down our hearts in the same way that excessive activities or exertions can encumber and cloud our minds. This is a serious warning!

✖ Describe in your own words how the heavy weight of anxieties has burdened your heart and the hearts of people close to you.

Anxiety is a heavy weight, but we're to throw all that weight into the mighty hand of God, who is more than able to carry it. And He wants to carry it because He cares for us! Let's go back to the helpful and wonderful words the apostle Peter wrote:

Humble yourselves, therefore, under the mighty hand of God so that at the proper time he may exalt you, casting all your anxieties on him, because he cares for you (1 Peter 5:6-7).

The Weight of Worry

In his exceptional wisdom given to him by God, King Solomon wrote, "Anxiety in a man's heart weighs him down" (Proverbs 12:25). Worry is like having a very heavy backpack strapped to your heart, forcing your feelings into sluggish weariness as you plod through life. You feel like it's impossible to ever attain the mountaintop and breathe deeply of the crisp, fresh air of joy.

Now you may be thinking, *I don't need Thelma to tell me that, and I don't need Solomon to say it either. I already know what a terrible burden being weighed down by worry is.* I hear you. Let's look at how Proverbs 12:25 ends: "Anxiety in a man's heart weighs him down, *but a good word makes him glad.*" There's a countermove to anxiety! Solomon says there's a solution, a cure! And it's relatively simple: a good word. Think about what that could mean for you as I share a big part of what that means to me.

> I once came close to having a nervous breakdown. I experienced fainting spells and disorientation. When I finally went to the doctor to see what was wrong, he wanted me to explain exactly what happened when I fainted. "Do you know what's going on around you while you're out?" he asked. "Can you hear people talking while you're out?" My answer to these questions was "yes." The doctor told me, "You didn't actually faint then. People who faint don't know what's going on around them."
>
> After further tests and visits with other specialists, they determined I was having some kind of mental episodes. And it was likely they would get worse if I didn't do something.
>
> One of the things my doctor asked me to do was to be careful about my self-talk. He emphasized how important

words are in dealing with our self-esteem. He told me to think positively about myself. And every time I thought or said something negative about myself, I was to immediately eradicate it with a positive. He even gave me a list of positive things to say!

Sometimes the negative way in which we habitually talk to ourselves becomes a breeding ground for anxieties to fester. So often we just need to change our self-talk a little bit—or maybe a lot.

We all talk to ourselves about ourselves, and when we do, we'd better watch what we're saying. You see, when we talk to ourselves, we invoke our consciousness. And in our conscious awareness, we truly hear what we say. Our subconscious hears it—and believes it! Then our creative self-consciousness gets busy working it out.

I'm told that if someone keeps telling himself or herself something negative (and untrue) for just 21 days, it will become true. That person will change and become what the self-talk said. And belief will eventually be reflected in behavior. I've heard people say:

- I can't do anything right.
- I just can't get anywhere on time.
- I'm so sick and tired of being sick and tired.
- I'm so clumsy, I don't know what to do.
- I'm so dumb…
- I'm so slow…

And I'm sure you can add to the list! Have you read the bumper sticker that says, "Life is hard…and then you die"? Pretty depressing, isn't it? Yes, people really say these things about themselves. Can you relate?

And once people get into this spiral of putdowns, it doesn't stop easily. The negative words we say and hear so easily drag us down. But the opposite is also true! Positive words will lift us up! Yes, that's the flipside: If we keep reminding ourselves of the things that are wonderful and true about us and affirm ourselves like that for just 21 days, our behavior will start to reflect our positive attitude. And if you have a difficult time coming up with some positives to say about you, I have some great suggestions!

Affirmations

I love affirmations. An affirmation is a positive statement spoken in the first-person singular, present tense, as if it's already true. (And it's something that *will* be true; that's what keeps it from being a lie.) If you will repeat affirmations to yourself often, you're on your way to feeling better because high self-esteem essentially centers on how you view yourself, which is reflected in the way you talk to yourself. Here are some great affirmations to tell yourself every day. I encourage you to jot them down and put them somewhere where you'll see them and be reminded of who you are in Christ.

- God loves me.
- God created me just as I am.
- God loves me so I love me too.
- Life will work out for me.
- I am healthy.
- I am blessed.
- I am loved by God and by people.
- My future is secure in Christ.
- I have a contribution to make to this world.
- In my heart and soul, I am forever young.
- I have all the money and resources I need.

Okay, did I hear laughter on that last one? I totally understand that. My point? If you keep telling yourself the wonderful truth, you allow God to move more freely and openly in you and your life. And if you work and do your part, He will certainly do His.

So if you need to, change the way you talk to yourself. And the right way of talking to yourself starts with the right thoughts in your mind. Yes, it's true that along with our intellect, our emotions and our wills (our hearts and souls) must also be involved. The critical start of this process is engaging the truth with our minds.

And to get the right thoughts inside our heads—to get the truth engraved there—God has given us His Word in strong, clear language so our minds can grasp hold of its truths.

A New Mind

When we're gripped by worries, we no longer see reality as it truly is. We see only a part of reality, and even that tends to be distorted. Ephesians 4:22-23 reveals something fundamental that can take place in our way of thinking: "Put off your old self...to be renewed in the spirit of your minds."

Isn't that amazing? Something revolutionary and transformational is possible in how we mentally process who we are and what our lives are all about. This invitation isn't that helpful for us if we don't understand how to get renewed. But now we know there *is a way* because God wouldn't have it in His Word for us if He won't help us achieve it.

In the next verse this wonderful opportunity for mental renewal is explained a bit more: "Put off your old self...to be renewed in the spirit of your minds, and to put on the new self, created after the likeness of God in true righteousness and holiness."

❈ Explain in your own words what this means and how it applies to your life.

❈ As you learn to more fully obey this verse, how will it help you become more dependent on God in healthy and helpful ways?

As you think about all the possibilities this mental renewal can mean for you, compare what you just read in Ephesians 4:23-24 with what's said in Romans 12:2:

> Do not be conformed to this world, but be transformed by the renewal of your mind, that by testing you may discern what is the will of God, what is good and acceptable and perfect.

🌼 What is most exciting to you about this kind of mental renewal God makes possible for you?

🌼 How do you think this process of mental transformation can help someone overcome anxiety?

🌼 How do you think you can best go about experiencing this transformation in your thoughts and attitudes?

🌼 What are the most significant things you've learned in this chapter about overcoming anxiety?

Remember This Reality: There's Something Better than Worry

We're making great progress! Let's review our four big realities:

Reality #1: God truly loves me, and He's fully committed to taking care of me and meeting my needs.

Reality #2: God is in complete control of my life. Whenever adverse circumstances inevitably come my way, I can know that my heavenly Father has allowed them to touch me. And I can know that He's totally able to lead me through those tough times to ultimate victory and wholeness and joy.

Reality #3: When I begin to anticipate the possibility of unpleasant circumstances in my life, I need to recognize that worry is a waste of time and energy. It's useless and pointless.

Reality #4: Prayer and thanksgiving are the most effective replacements for worry.

Are you all set to explore our fourth reality? Here it is expressed more fully:

I'm using worry in the right way
when I let it lead me to prayer and thanksgiving.
Prayerfulness and gratefulness are the best
replacements for anxiety.
Instead of anxiety and worry I can choose
peace and confidence in Christ.

Confidently Drawing Near

Sometimes our anxieties threaten to overwhelm us simply because we've forgotten (or don't really understand) the best steps to take in approaching God for help with the challenges and problems and troublesome possibilities that confront us now and in the future.

When we're tempted to worry and be anxious, whether it's a mild worry or a desperate need, God invites us to do something else instead. Hebrews 4:16 explains: "Let us then with confidence draw near to the throne of grace, that we may receive mercy and find grace to help in time of need."

✿ How well-established are you in seeking God's help? Practically speaking, in times of stress, what will help you remember you can draw near the throne of grace to receive mercy and grace?

✿ Do you have difficulty telling God what you need? If yes, what can you do to make it easier?

✿ When you draw near to God, do you fully expect to get help? To "receive mercy and find grace to help in time of need"? Why or why not?

✿ How can you effectively embrace the confidence to approach God when you're tempted to worry?

Our Privilege

We have the privilege of replacing our worry with prayer and with the peace of God. Next to being able to exchange our sins for the righteousness of Christ, I think this must be the most valuable and wonderful trade-off we could ever experience! Who wouldn't rather have prayerful intimacy and peace with God instead of the agitation and despair that accompanies anxiety?

Sometimes when we start to worry, the best advice is also the simplest:

Stop and pray!

The best and quickest way to do less worrying is simply to do more praying. Why is that true? Because real inner peace isn't the result of blindly ignoring your troubles, avoiding people you tend to get in conflicts with, or escaping into mindless entertainment. True peace is found in a personal, wholehearted encounter and conversation with God.

And it's so easy! If you can talk, you can pray! Praying is expressing yourself to God in whatever way you know how. I love the directness of David when he prayed:

> With my voice I cry out to the LORD;
>> with my voice I plead for mercy to the LORD.
> I pour out my complaint before him;
>> I tell my trouble before him
> (Psalm 142:1-2).

Anybody can do what David does in the book of Psalms. But there are some effective tools that may be helpful when we're praying, that may make it easier to open a conversation with God.

Pray the Word of God

Jesus is our example when it comes to how to deal with the temptations thrown at us by our enemy, Satan. When our Lord was tempted in the wilderness, after each temptation He said, "It is written…" and then quoted God's Word (Matthew 4:1-11). Jesus used Scripture to deflect the enemy's schemes. Likewise when we pray, praying the Word of God is a very effective tool.

Sometimes when people ask me to pray for them and I don't know the exact circumstances or the parties involved in their request, I pray the Word:

> Father, in the name of Jesus, I pray that [person's name] will trust in You with all his heart and lean not on his own understanding. In all his ways I pray he will acknowledge You, and I know You will direct his paths [Proverbs 3:5-6].

> Master Healer, I ask in Jesus' name that You will heal the cancer in [person's name]. Your Word reveals that You can heal every disease, for healing virtue can flow from Your body as it did when You healed the woman with the issue of blood. I stand on Your Word [Matthew 9:21].

> O Lord, my Provider, Your Word says that if I give according to Your Word, You will give back to me good measure, pressed down, shaken together, and running over. I trust this promise and expect the blessings. In Jesus' name [Luke 6:38].

There's power in praying the Word of God because His Word is everlasting. It will stay powerful and relevant throughout this world and the world to come.

Pray in Spirit and in Truth

We're taught in the Scriptures to pray in the Spirit without doubting and with confidence, believing that God will hear and answer our prayers. When we pray in truth, we come before our Master honestly and without pretense. Even if we're disappointed with God and wonder why our lives seem to be heading in an unwanted direction, we need to be authentic when we come before Him.

And when we pray in the Spirit, the Holy Spirit guides us in what to pray. (And He should never be ignored in this or in anything else.) Trust the Holy Spirit to help you pray the perfect will of the Father:

> The Spirit helps us in our weakness. For we do not know what to pray for as we ought, but the Spirit himself intercedes for us with groanings too deep for words. And he who searches hearts knows what is the mind of the Spirit, because the Spirit intercedes for the saints according to the will of God (Romans 8:26-27).

If we want to sap the strength out of our anxiety, we can't do it with sheer will-power. If we want to cripple our anxiousness and drain away its power, we need help from the Spirit of God. The Holy Spirit is our "worry quencher," our "fear fighter," our "anxiety crusher." He's truly our most constant encourager. Here's a practical example of how the Holy Spirit lifts us out of anxiety. Listen to what Jesus said to His followers:

> And when they bring you before the synagogues and the rulers and the authorities, do not be anxious about how you should defend yourself or what you should say, for the Holy Spirit will teach you in that very hour what you ought to say (Luke 12:11-12).

Now this was probably a very real comfort for the early believers. They knew what it was like to get dragged before the authorities and be threatened. Their faith in Christ and their witness for Christ often brought them into conflict with the political and religious powers of that time. Imprisonment and even death could be expected. With those prospects, who wouldn't be nervous and fearful if they found themselves being grilled by some court or council for the "crime" of proclaiming the good news of Jesus?

🌼 Imagine yourself in such a situation. (It might be a reality someday.)

What comfort would it bring if you knew the Holy Spirit would be there to teach you exactly how to answer every question?

❈ What can you do to ensure that your communication line with the Holy Spirit is wide open and available?

❈ In what other potentially anxious situations might you need to have the Holy Spirit teach you what to say?

❈ Write down a prayer asking for the Holy Spirit's help. Then thank the Holy Spirit for always being available, ready to assist you.

Pray with Gratitude

I mentioned in chapter 3 how God used Psalm 27 so mightily in my life to help me get through a painful period. God also gave me another passage that I live by every day: Philippians 4:6-7. I use these words from God constantly and find great comfort and strength in them.

I was drawn to these words from Philippians more than a decade ago when I asked God to show me the passage I would need more than any other in the coming year. I didn't know just how much I was going to need it until the first month of the year began with hurts and disappointments galore. Here's what Philippians 4:6-7 says:

> Do not be anxious about anything, but in everything by prayer and supplication with thanksgiving let your requests be made known to God. And the peace of God, which surpasses all understanding, will guard your hearts and your minds in Christ Jesus.

At first I had a hard time getting past the "with thanksgiving" part. I didn't understand why I was supposed to be giving thanks for being in a predicament. But with prayer and study I discovered a reason for giving thanks in everything: Before the world began, our sovereign God had *already worked out* everything that concerns us. We don't have to figure all this out; our job is to trust Him.

This Scripture has brought me much ease and contentment and spared me from getting thrashed by anxiety. It has kept me from crying all night, getting an upset stomach, having bouts of depression, talking angrily to someone, being impatient, and getting out of control. Or rather, it keeps me from these things when I remember what God says and follow His teachings.

Yes, sometimes I've found that the real battle starts when I get into a negative situation and remember to pull out of my arsenal of the Word of God to combat the situation. The spiritual warfare we talked about earlier is especially the battle for our minds. It's a deliberate attack from the devil. Using his demons, he tries to distract us from doing good, interfere with our righteous actions, demolish our godly relationships, dismantle our gifting, destroy the works of God's hands in our affairs, rearrange our godly desires, offend our witness as salt and light against evil, tarnish our good reputations, withhold our prosperity, ruin our health, strain our marriages, sabotage our ministries, disrespect our authorities, belittle our stand for right, defame our moral character, distort our proper business dealings, confuse our children, fracture our education, soil us with inappropriate legal matters, taint our friendly interactions, and overpower us with fear.

Jesus alone is the perfect defense against this onslaught. By prayer and thanksgiving we discover His peace that passes understanding, His peace that guards our hearts and minds in Him.

With that in mind, how wonderful to keep reflecting on these words: "Do not be anxious about anything" (Philippians 4:6).

Yes, it is possible to live free from anxiety.

Yes, it is possible to live at peace.

Are you ready for that? Then let Jesus do it! Let Him guard your heart and your mind.

Mary and Martha

Maybe Mary and Martha can help us out with this reality that there really is something better for us than anxiety—something we can consciously choose. Do you remember their story? To refresh your memory, let's go over it again from Luke 10:38-42.

Jesus and His disciples entered a village, and a woman named Martha invited them to her house.

So far, so good.

As a good hostess, Martha welcomes Jesus into her home. As she is bustling about preparing a meal and getting things ready, her sister, Mary, is listening to Jesus talk.

Mary gives her full attention to what Jesus has to say, and she sits humbly at His feet while doing so. In her culture this is how a disciple responds appropriately to his or her master and teacher.

Martha was distracted, working hard to get everything ready. Her willingness to serve isn't a bad attribute to have. Jesus said He "came not to be served but to serve" (Mark 10:45). Her intentions were doubtlessly good and she wanted to make her Lord comfortable and at ease in her home, but on this occasion her serving became a distraction. Her attention was being drawn away from something more important. What was it? Let's see. "And she went up to him and said, 'Lord, do you not care that my sister has left me to serve alone? Tell her then to help me'" (Luke 10:40).

If Martha had just quietly and contentedly continued straightening up the house and preparing the meal for her honored guest, would she have been commended by Jesus? I don't know. But one thing is for sure: By trying to pull her sister away from a teaching time with the Savior, Martha forced a comparison between her priorities and Mary's.

Plus, her absorption in her serving duties seems to have distorted her attitude toward the Lord. How she questioned the Lord seems unwise and inappropriate: "Do you not care…?" What is obviously uppermost in Martha's mind is herself, basically saying, "I have to do all the work myself. Is that fair? Mary should be helping me!" And isn't this exactly what anxiety tends to do? Get our focus on how *we're* being affected by a circumstance?

If you're like me, you've wondered what the Lord was talking about with His disciples and Mary when Martha interrupted them. Can you imagine how wise and wonderful and inspiring His words were—and yet Martha misses out on all that and even interrupts the teaching moment. "You need to pay attention to me for a minute, Lord," she's saying basically. "I've got work to do, and Mary needs to help me, and that's more important than what she's been doing and what You've been telling her. Tell her to help me!"

Anxiety blinds us like that sometimes, doesn't it? We can't see past our own preoccupations.

The Lord answered, "Martha, Martha, you are anxious and troubled about many things, but one thing is necessary. Mary has chosen the good portion, which will not be taken away from her" (Luke 10:41-42).

The Lord Jesus shows understanding and concern for Martha's situation. He is kind and respectful in how He speaks to her. He doesn't rail at her by saying, "Quit your fussin' and sit down like your sister here!" He knows Martha has a lesson to learn from Mary in this moment, and Jesus says it like it is without belittling her or using sarcasm.

🌸 Reflect on Jesus' words to Martha, and then explain the lesson she needed to learn.

🌸 Do your priorities play a decisive part in whether you experience anxiety? Why or why not?

- In your experience, how can anxiety be lessened by giving priority to spending time in the Word of God and taking in the Lord's teaching?

- Do you think being released from anxiety requires a conscious choice on your part (like the choice Mary made)? Why or why not?

Staying worried in any situation is ultimately a matter of choice, of making a decision. Worrying means we're choosing to *not* trust God and to *not* believe He has everything under control, including the details of our present and future. And yes, we'll need to make the decision to *not* worry and *to trust God* over and over again because we're human and have human limitations. So will you make this your decision of choice? "I choose not to worry over this situation. Instead, I choose to believe that God will do what is in my best interests."

- What will it take for you to make this decision when you're in a situation that tends to make you really anxious?

- What will making this decision look like in your life? In other words, what steps will you take as you make the decision and after you make the decision?

What's Ahead?

As you look ahead, what do you see in terms of worry and anxiety? Let's return once more to David's recorded words in Psalm 138:

> I give you thanks, O LORD, with my whole heart;
> > before the gods I sing your praise;
> I bow down toward your holy temple
> > and give thanks to your name for your
> > > steadfast love and your faithfulness,
> for you have exalted above all things
> > your name and your word.
> On the day I called, you answered me;
> > my strength of soul you increased.
> All the kings of the earth shall give you thanks, O LORD,
> > for they have heard the words of your mouth,
> and they shall sing of the ways of the LORD,
> > for great is the glory of the LORD.
> For though the LORD is high, he regards the lowly,
> > but the haughty he knows from afar.
> Though I walk in the midst of trouble,
> > you preserve my life;
> you stretch out your hand against the wrath of my enemies,
> > and your right hand delivers me.
> The LORD will fulfill his purpose for me;
> > your steadfast love, O LORD, endures forever.
> > Do not forsake the work of your hands.

Yes, David was quite familiar with affliction and distress. Did you catch the last few sentences he wrote and sang?

> Though I walk in the midst of trouble,
> > you preserve my life...
> your right hand delivers me (verse 7).

Since David was assured that his life would be preserved and that the Lord's right hand would deliver him, he also sang the next verse for all the world to hear:

The LORD will fulfill his purpose for me;
your steadfast love, O LORD, endures forever.

✿ How convinced are you that the Lord will fulfill His purpose for
you? What do you base that on?

✿ What do you think that purpose is?

David, in his great confidence, added this final plea to the Lord:

Do not forsake the work of your hands (verse 8).

Will this also be *your* confidence in God and *your* prayer to Him?
It can be! Yes, that's your privilege for as long as you live, in whatever
situation you find yourself.

✿ Express David's attitude in Psalm 138 in your own words as a
testament to the Lord and your assurance of victory over anxiety
in Him.

✿ What are the most significant things you've learned in this chapter
about overcoming anxiety?

Notes

Chapter 1: Analyzing Anxiety

1. All quotes from Dr. Hart are taken from Dr. Archibald D. Hart, "Anxiety," in *The Complete Book of Everyday Christianity: An A-to-Z Guide to Following Christ in Every Aspect of Life*, Robert Banks and R. Paul Stevens, eds. (Downers Grove, IL: InterVarsity Press, 1997).

2. Psychology Information Online, http://www.psychologyinfo.com/problems/anxiety.html, Donald J. Franklin, Ph.D., dev., copyright © 1999, 2000, 2002, 2003. All rights reserved. Accessed Oct. 2009.

Chapter 2: The Fear In Anxiety

1. Psychology Information Online, http://www.psychologyinfo.com/problems/anxiety.html, Donald J. Franklin, Ph.D., dev., copyright © 1999, 2000, 2002, 2003. All rights reserved. Accessed Oct. 2009.

2. Hebrews 12:2 NKJV.

Chapter 5: Remember This Reality: God Is Able

1. Neil S. Wilson, ed., *The Handbook of Bible Application* (Eastbourne, England: Kingsway, 1993 / WordSearch Corp., database 2007), accessed 2009.

Chapter 6: Remember This Reality: Worry Is a Waste

1. Neil S. Wilson, ed., *The Handbook of Bible Application* (Eastbourne, England: Kingsway, 1993 / WordSearch Corp., database 2007), accessed 2009.

About the Author

THELMA WELLS' life has been a courageous journey of faith. Born to an unwed and physically disabled teenager, the name on Thelma's birth certificate read simply "Baby Girl Morris." Her mother worked as a maid in the "big house" while they lived in the servants' quarters. When Thelma stayed at her grandparents' home, her grandmother locked her in a dark, smelly, insect-infested closet all day. To ease her fear, Thelma sang every hymn and praise song she knew.

A trailblazer for black women, Thelma worked in the banking industry and was a professor at Master's International School of Divinity. Her vivacious personality and talent for storytelling attracted the attention of the Women of Faith Conference. She was soon one of their core speakers. She was named Extraordinary Woman of the Year in 2008 by the Extraordinary Women Conferences. She also received the Advanced Writers and Speakers Association's Lifetime Achievement Award in 2009.

Along with writing books, including *Don't Give In...God Wants You to Win!* Thelma is president of Woman of God Ministries. "Mama T," as she is affectionately known, helps girls and women all over the world discover Jesus and live for Him.

Thelma earned degrees at North Texas State University and Master's International School of Divinity. She was awarded an honorary Doctorate of Divinity (DD) from St. Thomas Christian College and Theological Seminary and ordained through the Association of Christian Churches in Florida.

Thelma and George, her husband of 48 years, enjoy spending time with their children, grandchildren, and great-grandchildren.

For more information about Thelma and her ministry, check out
www.thelmawells.com.

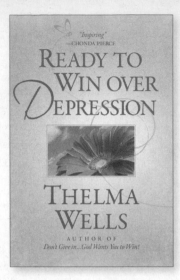

"Inspiring"
—CHONDA PIERCE

READY TO WIN OVER DEPRESSION

THELMA WELLS

AUTHOR OF
Don't Give in...God Wants You to Win!

You don't have to feel good or positive to start this book.
You are not alone or crazy.
You can start winning over depression today!

Has sadness taken over? Have you talked, prayed, and even focused on "happy thoughts" but continue to slog through every day? Popular author Thelma Wells has been there. She knows it's hard to start down the recovery road, but she did... and reached the promised land of hope and joy. And she wants to help you do the same.

Sharing personal stories along with God's wisdom, Thelma invites you to join her on an easy-to-read journey out of depression. Interactive questions let you explore where you're at, and biblical insights and practical suggestions show you how to counter life's negativity by...

- discovering why God created you and loves you
- uncovering the positive truths about who you are
- developing a better knowledge of how Jesus can help you
- finding caring people who will listen and offer godly advice
- caring for yourself spiritually, emotionally, and physically

Thelma is a great traveling companion and encourager, making your path to good health positive and steady.

God Calls You "Winner"!

Is stress, indecision, heartache, or fear zapping your energy? Popular speaker and author Thelma Wells says life doesn't have to be that way! Opening her heart and God's Word, she reveals how God taught her to stand tall to win against discouragement and oppression by putting on God's armor. You'll discover...

- what spiritual warfare is
- who you're fighting
- what you're accomplishing

Thelma's contagious energy and enthusiasm invite you to tackle life with a "can do" attitude. You'll find great ways to dress for successful spiritual battle by:

- fixing your hair
  (putting on the helmet of salvation in Jesus for safety)
- padding your heart
  (donning the breastplate of righteousness to confront evil)
- putting on your stomping shoes
  (stepping out in faith against the devil)

No human wins every fight, so Thelma encourages you to call on Jesus when you get tired. He wants you to win, and He actively participates with you to ensure victory.

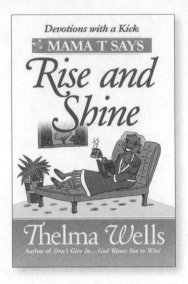

It's a Brand-new Day!

Dynamic, upbeat, and forthright, author and popular speaker Thelma "Mama T" Wells encourages you to choose joy every day…and explains how to do that even when trouble turns your world upside down.

Through biblical wisdom and powerful stories that highlight God's amazing presence, extraordinary love, and unfailing provision, you'll soon embrace Thelma's steps to welcoming each day:

- never say "never" to God
- love and spend time with your family and friends
- be liberal with praise
- talk to God about everything
- dig into God's Word

From simple strategies to in-depth approaches, Mama T shows you how to draw closer to Jesus, experience the help He offers, and put joy and contentment into your day.

Notes

Notes

Notes

Notes

Notes

Notes

Notes

Notes

Notes

Notes

Notes

Notes